Beyond the Tyranny of the Majority
Voting Methodologies in Decision-making and Electoral Systems

*"Consensus Voting Systems"*, published in 1991 as a *'samizdat'*.
*"The Politics of Consensus"*, 1994, a second *'samizdat'*.

*"Beyond the Tyranny of the Majority*
*Voting Methodologies in Decision-making and Electoral Systems"*
ISBN 0 9506028 5 X

## Published by THE DE BORDA INSTITUTE

Copyright © Peter Emerson 1998
THE DE BORDA INSTITUTE
36 Ballysillan Road
Belfast BT14 7QQ

Those who use any information contained in this book
are asked to give all due credits.

*This book has received support from the Cultural Traditions Programme of the*
*Community Relations Council, which aims to encourage acceptance and*
*understanding of cultural diversity. The views expressed do not necessarily*
*reflect those of the NI Community Relations Council.*

THE DE BORDA INSTITUTE *is devoted to the promotion of inclusive voting*
*procedures, especially in societies which must enjoy religious and/or ethnic*
*diversity if they are to survive. The Institute has been funded by the Joseph*
*Rowntree Charitable Trust.*

Typeset by the author
at Community Computer Resource Centre
Hazelwood College, Belfast

Printed by Colour Image, Lucan

*"However democratic simple majority [decision-making] initially appears to be, it cannot in fact be so."*\*

\* *"Liberalism and Populism"* by W H Riker, 1982, p 65.

# BEYOND THE TYRANNY OF THE MAJORITY

## VOTING METHODOLOGIES IN DECISION-MAKING AND ELECTORAL SYSTEMS

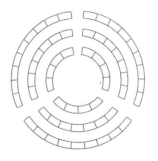

by

P. J. EMERSON

*"In representative government, not only is it possible that power will be seized by cunning, immoral, and artful mediocrities, such as various prime ministers and presidents have been, but the construction of these governments is such that only that kind of people can obtain power."*

**Lev Tolstoy** writing in
*"The meaning of the Russian revolution"*,
section V, first published in 1906.

---

List of abbreviations

| | | |
|---|---|---|
| AMS | = | additional member system |
| AV | = | alternative vote. |
| DUP | = | Democratic Unionist Party |
| EU | = | European Union |
| GNU | = | Government of National Unity |
| GP | = | Green Party |
| Lab | = | Labour Party |
| Lib | = | Liberal or Liberal Democrat Party |
| MMP | = | mixed member proportional |
| NI | = | Northern Ireland |
| NIO | = | Northern Ireland Office |
| OSCE | = | Organisation for Security & Co-operation in Europe |
| OUP | = | Oxford University Press |
| PR | = | proportional representation |
| PUP | = | Progressive Unionist Party |
| QBS | = | quota Borda system |
| SDLP | = | Social Democratic and Labour Party |
| SNP | = | Scottish National Party |
| SF | = | Sinn Féin |
| STV | = | single transferable vote |
| UDP | = | Ulster Democratic Party |
| UK | = | United Kingdom |
| UKUP | = | United Kingdom Unionist Party |
| USA | = | United States of America |
| USSR | = | Union of Soviet Socialist Republics |
| UUP | = | Ulster Unionist Party |

NB      All quotes are given with the emphases of their original authors.

# CONTENTS

# GLOSSARY

**ABSOLUTE MAJORITY**
An option or candidate has an absolute as opposed to a simple or relative majority if it enjoys at least 50% of the vote.

**ADDITIONAL MEMBER SYSTEM (AMS)**
Allows for some representatives to be elected directly via a first-past-the-post election, and others via a top-up.

**ALTERNATIVE VOTE (AV)**
A form of STV used when only one result is required; this is obviously the case when STV is used in decision-making, but STV can also be used for elections in single-member constituencies, in which case, of course, it is not proportional.

**APPROVAL VOTING**
A variation of majority voting designed primarily for elections; voters 'approve' of one or more candidates, and those candidates which thus gain the highest 'majorities' of approvals are then deemed elected.

**ARROW'S THEOREM**
Arrow's 'General Possibility Theorem' suggests no one voting procedure can be absolutely fair; (please see p 94).

**BORDA COUNT**
This is a points system where, in say a 6-option ballot, the voter gives 5 points to his favourite option/candidate, 4 points to his second choice, and so on, with 1 point for his penultimate choice. The option(s)/candidates with the highest points total is/are deemed to be the outcome.

**BORDA PREFERENDUM**
The preferendum count is just a little different from the above, the punter now giving 6 points to her favourite option/candidate, 5 points to her second choice, and so on, down to a 1 point for her ultimate choice. See also partial voting and preferendum.

**CARDINAL PREFERENCES**
Cardinal preferences are weighted, as for example when one child says '*I like the zoo ten times as much as the seaside,' whereupon the other retorts, 'Well, I like the seaside a hundred times as much as the zoo. So there!*' (McLean, 1989, p 52.).

**CONDORCET** (*pronounced 'kondoorsay'*)
The Condorcet system asks the voter to list all the options/candidates in his/her order of preference. The count compares each pair of options/candidates in turn, and that option/candidate which wins every pairing is termed a Condorcet winner.

**CONSENSORS**
A team of, say, three independent non-voting persons whose task on any controversial issue is to draw up a list of options to represent the diversity of opinions expressed in debate, and once the agreement of those participants to that list has been received, to present this (modified) list as the ballot paper for a preferendum.

**CONSENSUS**
The Concise Oxford Dictionary offers two opposites: either *"general agreement"* or *"majority view"*. Others use the term to infer unanimity. In this work, the word relates to that option with which all (or almost all) agree to compromise. In the NI Talks, the term *"sufficient consensus"* is used to describe the support of majorities in both (or all three) groupings: unionists, nationalists (and non-aligned).

**CONSENSUS, LEVEL OF**
This term is applicable to the preferendum; it is the number of points gained by an option expressed as a percentage of the maximum possible number of points any option could gain. That is, an option's level of consensus is the measure of the overall level of support among the voters for that particular option.

**CONSOCIATIONAL VOTING**
Refers to a majority vote taken simultaneously in two or more separate constituencies.

**CYCLE OR CYCLICAL MAJORITY,** see paradox.

**DEMOCRACY**
If by democracy we mean *"government of the people, by the people, and for the people"* - to quote Abraham Lincoln's 1863 Gettysburg address - we must define the decision-making methodology by which such government is to be effected. Only then might all the people be involved rather than just some of them, and to that end, this book is dedicated.

**D'HONDT**
A divisor system of counting used in some PR-list elections with divisors 1, 2, 3, 4...

**DIVISOR SYSTEM**
A way of calculating which party is to get how many seats in a PR-list electoral system. Every candidate's vote total is divided by a series of specific numbers (which vary according to the particular divisor system in use), and seats are awarded to the highest resultant scores. The main divisors are d'Hondt, St. Lague and Modified St. Lague.

**DROOP**
The quota used in some PR-list, nearly all PR-STV, and QBS elections. It is the first integer greater than {the valid vote} divided by {the number of representatives to be elected plus one}.

**ELECTORATE**
The total number of persons eligible to vote.

## EXCLUSIVE
A voting procedure is exclusive if the outcome depends on only some of the voters, and even then, on only their first preferences.

## FAIR
A voting procedure may be considered fair if the outcome from the subsequent count accurately reflects the voters' 'sincere' wishes, (see p xiv).

## FIRST-PAST-THE-POST
The simple or relative majority 'x' vote, in which the candidate with the most votes wins (whether or not he/she reaches any 'post'). It is otherwise known as a plurality vote.

## GENDER QUOTAS
These may be applied to most electoral systems, and the better procedure is to ask any party nominating 2, 3 (or more) candidates to ensure that at least, say, 1 (or 40%) of the candidates are male/female. Whether or not the voters choose a balanced number is of course up to them, but experience in Scandinavia suggests that the electorate soon gets used to mixed representation.

## HARE
A quota used in some PR-list elections; it is obtained by dividing {the valid vote} by {the number of representatives} to be elected.

## IMPERIALI
A quota based on {the valid vote} divided by {the number of representatives to be elected plus two}.

## INCLUSIVE
A voting procedure is inclusive if the outcome of the subsequent count is influenced by all the preferences cast by all of those voting.

## IRRELEVANT ALTERNATIVE
This term is used to describe an option which, because of the voting procedure to be used, is not strictly pertinent, either to the subsequent vote, and therefore perhaps, or to the debate itself. The inclusion of such an option, even though every voter and every participant in the debate considers it to be less popular than one of the other contenders, may nevertheless affect the result.

## LIST
Most PR-list electoral systems allow the voter only one preference from a list of candidates drawn up by each of the contending parties; either a divisor or a quota is used in the count.

## MAJORITARIAN
A decision-making process is said to be majoritarian and adversarial if the success of any one proposal depends only on the strength of support for that option by those in favour relative to the support of other persons for any other options.

**MAJORITARIANISM**
The belief which usually relates to the idea that a majority has the right to rule.

**MAJORITY NUMBER**
A variation of the Condorcet count; it is used to establish the outcome when there is no obvious Condorcet winner.

**MAJORITY VOTING**
(See also relative or simple, absolute, and weighted majority, as well as first-past-the-post.) The voter is allowed to write one 'x', and the highest score wins.

**MATRIX VOTE**
This voting procedure may be used whenever an electorate wishes to elect a definite number of persons to the same number of specific posts as, for example, when a parliament elects a government.

Now a minister of agriculture presumably requires talents different from those felt advantageous for a chancellor of the exchequer, yet both need to be elected in the one procedure. The matrix vote enables every member of parliament to award preferendum points to his chosen favourites, in his order of preference, at the same time stating in which post he wishes each to serve.

The matrix vote is based on a QBS count, so the answer will be a representative, proportional, power-sharing, all-party coalition, a government of national unity (GNU).

**MODIFIED ST. LAGUE**
A divisor count for use in PR-list voting; it uses the divisors 1.4, 3, 5, 7...

**MONOTONICITY**
That property of a voting procedure which means that if an option/candidate becomes more popular, it/he/she will have a greater chance of success. Surprisingly enough, not every system can actually guarantee this.

**MULTI-MEMBER CONSTITUENCY**
In PR elections, more than one representative will be elected, so these sorts of elections are held in multi-member as opposed to single-member constituencies.

**ORDINAL PREFERENCES**
Are placed 1st, 2nd, 3rd, etc., unlike cardinal preferences. See also utility function.

**PARADOX OF VOTING**
When three or more people discuss three or more options, there may often be no one single option which is more popular than both or all the other options. This leads to the situation where, say, 'A' is more popular than 'B', which is more popular than 'C', which is more popular than 'A'... and where, therefore, one goes round and round in circles.

A paradox can often occur in any binary, majoritarian voting procedure involving a minimum of three persons and at least three options/candidates, if and when that procedure allows the voters to state their preferences.

PARETO OPTIMAL
This suggests that if everyone in society prefers something, then the voting procedure or social choice function should not come up with something else.

PARTIAL VOTE
In multi-option voting , a voter may either complete a full ballot paper, or hand in a partially completed paper, or again, abstain.

In the preferendum, the voter's level of participation in the democratic process is determined by her level of participation in the vote. In contrast, in PR-STV, the voter's 1st preference has a full value, regardless of how many other preferences she records.

PLURALIST
A democracy may be said to be pluralist if it manages to sustain more than two 'main' parties. A voting system may be pluralist if it allows the voter to cast preferences for more than one candidate of more than one party.

PLURALITY
This name is sometimes used to describe 'first-past-the-post' voting, i.e., 'majority' voting on a plurality of candidates (or options). The voter puts an 'x' opposite his favourite, and the winner is that candidate who enjoys in some cases a majority of the votes, in other instances, only the largest minority.

PREFERENCE VOTING
In preference voting, a voter records her 1st preference and may also record her 2nd and subsequent preferences.

PREFERENDUM
This is a decision-making process which involves a debate, a vote according to the rules laid down for a preferendum count (see below), and an analysis of that vote. See also Appendix VI.

PREFERENDUM COUNT
This is conducted according to the rules of a Borda count, with a variation of those rules on any partial votes.

In a preferendum of $n$ options (or candidates) where $n$ is not a large number, voters may vote for one, some or all the options listed by casting $n$ points for their most favoured option, $n-1$ for their next favourite, $n-2$ for their third choice, and so on; those who so wish may submit a completed ballot paper, casting 2 points for their penultimate choice and 1 point for their least favoured option.

Where $n$ is a large number, voters may be asked to vote for only $m$ options (or candidates), casting $m$ points for their most favoured option, $m-1$ for their next favourite, and so on.

This is particularly useful when using the preferendum to produce a short list of say six options (or candidates) from an initial choice of 20 or more, either in a social survey, or as a straw poll to assist a decision-making process or as the final stage of that process, or again in an election.

In this instance, of course, $m = 6$.

#### Proportional representation, (PR)

There are a number of election systems which give a measure of proportional representation, some more than others. Many countries use PR-list systems, most of which allow the voter to express only one preference. Other forms of PR include PR-STV and QBS.

#### Qualified majority voting

The system used in the EU: France, Germany, Italy and the UK have 10 votes each; Spain has 8; Belgium, Greece, the Netherlands and Portugal have 5; Austria and Sweden have 4; Denmark, Finland and Ireland 3, and Luxembourg 2. A qualified majority vote is passed if it gets at least 62 of the 87 possible.

#### Quota

The number of votes required to obtain a seat in some PR electoral systems; there are two main types, the Droop and the Hare quotas.

#### Quota Borda system (QBS)

An electoral system in which voters award preference points to one, some or all the candidates, standing in multi-member constituencies.

For an *n*-candidate constituency, the voter gives *n* points to her/his most preferred candidate, *n-1* to her next favourite, *n-2* to her third choice, and so on, as in a preferendum vote.

The count starts by:

a)  calculating a Droop quota for the number of valid votes cast;
b)  recording the number of each candidate's first preferences, and
c)  adding each candidate's total points from all preferences cast, to get each candidate's preferendum total.

The count is conducted in four stages:

1   Any candidates whose first preference score equals or exceeds the quota is elected.
2   If there are seats still to be filled, the count enters the second stage where candidates are considered in pairs, as follows. Every pair of candidates is examined - 'AB, AC, AD'... 'BC, BD'... etc. - and the number of voters for each pair of candidates such as 'A and D' for whom voters vote either 'A' first and 'D' second or 'D' first and 'A' second, is totalled. Any 'pair' gaining the quota is awarded a seat, the successful candidate being the one from the pair with the higher preferendum total.
3   The third stage is similar to the second. If seats are still to be filled, candidates are considered in triplets such as 'C, F and K', where voters vote *n*, *n-1* and *n-2* for these three candidates, in no matter what order. Any such 'triplet' gaining the quota is awarded a seat, and the successful candidate is again the one from the triplet with the highest preferendum total.

In both the second and third stages, only those pairs and triplets which do not include a candidate who has already been elected are considered.

4   In the fourth and final stage, any remaining seats are awarded to those candidates with the highest preferendum totals.

## REFERENDUM

A voting process usually based on a choice of only two options; the old status quo and the new proposal. A referendum can, however, be multi-optional, as has happened in Newfoundland and Sweden, for example. Two-option referendums are counted by simple or weighted majority vote; multi-option referendums are usually counted in two-round majority votes, though in theory they could be conducted by alternative vote, Condorcet or preferendum methodologies.

## RIGHT OF SELF-DETERMINATION

This is a right as ill-defined as the term 'democracy', for no 'self' should be able to determine itself on the basis of only a majority of itself.

## ST. LAGUE

A divisor count for use in PR-list voting; it uses the divisors 1, 3, 5, 7...

## SIMPLE OR RELATIVE MAJORITY

An option or candidate has a simple or relative majority if it or he/she has a majority of the votes in a two-option/candidate ballot, or the largest minority in a multi-option/candidate poll, respectively.

## SINCERE VOTING

A person votes sincerely (as opposed to tactically) if she lists her preferences exactly as she wants to, without taking other factors into consideration.

## SINGLE TRANSFERABLE VOTE (STV)

This is used in AV and PR-STV. The voter puts a 1 opposite his 1st choice, and may also place a 2/3/... opposite his 2nd/3rd/... favourites. In AV, the quota is 50% + 1, and any option/candidate gaining the quota is deemed adopted/elected. In PR-STV, the quota is usually based on the Droop formula; any candidate(s) gaining that quota is/are also elected, and any surplus in excess of the quota is transferred in accordance with the voters' subsequent preferences. If in AV no one option/candidate gains the quota, or if in PR-STV there are seats still to be filled, the least popular option/candidate is eliminated and again the votes are transferred in accordance with the voters' subsequent preferences. The process continues until, in AV, an option/candidate gains the quota, or in PR-STV, until the full number of seats has been allocated.

## SOCIAL CHOICE FUNCTION

A means of deciding what society should have, on the basis of knowing what every member of that society wants; in other words, a social choice function is usually a voting procedure, but the ancient Greeks for example preferred a lottery.

## TACTICAL VOTING

A person is said to vote tactically if, instead of voting sincerely, she adjusts her preferences because of some tactical consideration. In a UK election, for instance, a Liberal supporter may nevertheless vote Labour, just to get the Tories out. As a general rule, the more sophisticated the voting system, the more difficult it is to manipulate in this way, though no system is perfect.

THRESHOLD
i)   For most electoral systems, its threshold is the approximate percentage of (1st preference) votes required to ensure minimum electoral success.
ii)  The term can also be used in relation to the minimum level required in any top-up system; the Germans, for example, have a 5% threshold, originally concocted by the occupying powers to keep out the communists!

TOP-UP
A top-up election is usually carried out for the same purpose as a two-tier election, namely, to ensure overall proportionality. Representatives are elected in their own constituencies, but the same votes are then counted on a regional or national basis, and further seats are awarded to those parties not yet fairly represented.

TWO-TIER SYSTEMS
A two-tier or dual-vote electoral system is one which uses two different systems, so to combine the advantages of one with those of another. In Sweden, for instance, the first (PR-list) vote is counted in small local multi-member constituencies, so as to ensure a degree of geographical intimacy between the representatives and the electorate, and the second count is conducted in (a few regional, or one national) large constituency(ies), to guarantee a good degree of overall proportionality.

TURNOUT
The number or percentage of the electorate which votes.

UTILITY FUNCTION
A term used in any points system to describe the relationship between the points awarded to a favourite option and those awarded to any subsequent choices. In most cases, and most certainly whenever the Borda count or preferendum is being used, the utility function is 1, i.e., preferences are ordinal. Whether in, say, a 6-option preferendum, points awarded are '6, 5, 4, 3, 2, 1' or '5, 4, 3, 2, 1, 0 ' matters little; if, however, they are '10, 6, 4, 3, 2, 1' as in Grand-Prix motor racing, then you might well get a different champion.

VALID VOTE
The turnout minus any invalid votes.

VETO
This is a device, sometimes referred to as a 'right', which applies to nearly all majoritarian decision-making processes, but it is certainly no more 'right' than the other wrong, the right of majority rule.

VOTING PROFILE
The various preferences of those concerned.

WEIGHTED VOTING
For any proposal to be approved when using weighted majority voting, it must get not just a simple or absolute majority, but a particular weighting like 2/3rds of the valid vote.

# FOREWORD

At first glance, Peter Emerson's book might look like a mere survey of different voting procedures, setting out their advantages and disadvantages: different methods of voting on committees in Chapter 1, and different electoral systems in Chapter 2. It is nothing so tame. It is an impassioned ideological manifesto: it argues vehemently for the author's conception of what democracy should be understood to be, and against a widespread misconception of what democracy is.

How can an impassioned ideological manifesto be filled with tables showing the outcomes of votes and of elections in hypothetical cases under this or that system? The question rests upon one of the misconceptions that must be cleared away. The misconception is that the choice of a voting procedure or of an electoral system is merely the selection of a mechanism for doing what we are all agreed needs to be done. Of course, if we define 'what needs to be done' in too mechanical a way, then the choice *can* be characterised in this way. It can be so characterised if we describe the choice of a voting procedure by a council or committee as a way of determining how the council or committee is to act, and if we characterise an electoral system as a way of determining who shall sit in Parliament. But as soon as we ask by what criteria or in accordance with what principles these things should be decided, the appearance that we are merely selecting a mechanism for doing what we are all agreed has to be done vanishes.

By what criteria or in accordance with what principles should it be determined what a council or committee should do, in the light of the judgements of its members? By what criteria or in accordance with what principles should it be determined who is fitted to sit in Parliament as representing a constituency, in the light of the preferences of the constituents between the candidates? By what criteria or in accordance with what principles should it be determined how Parliament is to be divided among the political parties, in the light of the preferences of the electors between the parties? A particular voting procedure or a particular electoral system attempts to translate into the mechanism of decision certain such principles and certain such criteria. It may fail to translate them faithfully, and such a failure is important. But what are far more important are the principles and criteria that it is attempting to embody. It is these with which Peter Emerson is primarily concerned.

When a council adopts a voting procedure, it is implicitly sanctioning certain principles as governing how a communal decision ought to be arrived at, given the opinions of the individuals concerned: for the voting procedure is designed to function according to those principles. Likewise, when a Parliament decrees the use of a particular electoral system, it is endorsing a certain conception of who should be considered as representative of a given constituency, and of what the composition of parliament should be, given the opinions and preferences of the electorate. A voting procedure and an electoral system are not, therefore, mere pieces of mechanism: they enshrine general ideals of what democracy is.

A widespread conception of democracy is that it consists in realising the wishes of the majority. To this conception Peter Emerson is deeply opposed. Why do people believe this, and why does Emerson disagree?

One reason why people believe it, is that they constantly hear it said. It is commonplace to hear, *"We're doing it because a majority is in favour of it: that's democracy, isn't it?"* The British and Irish governments are united in declaring that no change will be made to how Northern Ireland is governed unless a majority of the population favours it. The implication is that whatever change a majority favours will be made: it will be no matter what the minority wants.

But how did people come to think like this in the first place? Well, as Emerson points out, there is nothing else to think when the choice that confronts us is a *binary* one: that is, when the only options are to do 'A' or to do 'Z', or simply to do 'A' or not to do 'A'. If that really is the choice, then there is nothing for it but to adopt whichever of the two options the majority prefers. But, as Peter Emerson insists, it is very seldom that there are only two possible options before us. Between doing 'A' and doing 'Z' there may well be intermediate compromise options, 'B, M or Y'. He believes that true democracy demands that whenever, for each of two options, there is a body of opinion strongly opposed to it, a compromise should be sought, even if there is a slim majority in favour of one of the two. The principle of democracy is not, in his view, that a majority should always be given its way: it is, rather, that decisions should not ride rough-shod over the wishes of minorities, even when they accord with the wishes of a majority. He thinks, indeed, that the mechanism of decision should require that no decision should be made final if it proves that there is sufficiently strong opposition to it on the part of a sizeable minority. If this is found to be the case, then it should be mandatory to resort to further discussion, for the purpose of arriving at a compromise solution.

But how are we to tell how strong the opposition is to a particular option on the part of those voters who do not support it? If a binary vote is held, each voter having to vote for one of just two options, we cannot tell. Emerson believes that the belief that the object of democracy is to realise the will of the majority leads to the use of methods of voting that artificially represent all votes as binary. For instance, when there are three possible options, 'A, B and C', one well-known method is first to vote between two of them, say 'A and B', and then take a vote between the winning option out of those two and the remaining option 'C'.

Suppose that a voter votes for 'B' on the first ballot, which 'B' wins; he then votes again for 'B' on the second ballot between 'B and C'. We know that he prefers 'B to C', but we have no way of knowing how strongly. We do not know whether he would have preferred 'A to C' or 'C to A'; we cannot even be certain he prefers 'B to A'. For his vote for 'B' on the first ballot might have been tactical: if, for example, he thought that 'C' would beat 'A' on the second ballot, and his preference for 'B over C' was strong. Such a method of voting places someone whose preference is for 'A over B' and 'B over C', or of for 'C over B' and 'B over A', in a difficult position to know how to vote on the first ballot to achieve the result that is optimal for him.

How, then, is it possible to discover the strengths of voters' preferences? They will be revealed in some measure if there are several options to be voted on simultaneously, and voters are asked to fill their ballot papers in the way in which Emerson believes that they should be. They should be asked to do what is familiar to voters in both parts of Ireland, namely to number the options in order of preference.

If, out of five options, a voter indicates that he prefers 'A to B, B to M, M to Y and Y to Z', then we may take it that he has a mild preference for 'A over B', but a strong preference for 'A over Z'. Peter Emerson argues for a system, which he calls the preferendum, in which such ballot papers are used in the following manner to allocate point-scores to the options.

Suppose there are five options, 'A, B, M, Y and Z'. Each voter is asked to contribute 5 points to his favourite option, 4 points to his second preference, 3 to his next choice, 2 to his penultimate option and 1 to the option he ranks the lowest. The one with the highest point-total is the winner.

Let us see how the preferendum works. Suppose there are 1000 voters, of whom 520 rank the options in the order:

A
B
M
Y
Z

Another 80 rank them in the order

M
Y
B
Z
A

The remaining 400 rank them in the order

Z
Y
M
B
A

Here 'A' is the first choice of 52% of the voters, a clear majority. But 'A' is a divisive option; all the other 48% of the voters rank it lowest. 'Z' is also a divisive option: 40% of the voters rank it highest, but 8% rank it lowest but one and 52% rank it lowest of all. The preferendum scores of the options will be:

| A | B | M | Y | Z |
|------|------|------|------|------|
| 3080 | 3120 | 3160 | 2960 | 2680 |

'A' has an absolute majority of first preferences, but 'M' has the highest preferendum score.

In a case like this, many theorists would wish 'M' to win outright. But 'M', though an uncontentious option, is a mediocre one; its score is not greatly above the average (3000). For Peter Emerson, this would be an instance in which further discussion was needed to see if 'M', or any new compromise suggestion, could obtain a high measure of general support. 'M' has what Emerson calls a level of consensus of just over 63%, defined as the ratio of the outcome's actual preferendum score to the highest possible preferendum score (here 5000). Emerson would be reluctant to allow an outright victory, without further discussion, to an outcome with a level of consensus no higher than that.

The essential idea of the preferendum is due to a French theorist, Jean-Charles de Borda, who wrote in the period just preceding the French

Revolution. It is a remarkable truth that he and a contemporary, the Maquis de Condorcet, discovered what remain today the fundamental facts concerning the theory of voting. It will be seen that, under the preferendum, an option which is the first choice of a majority of the voters may not get the highest score: those first choices may be offset by its being the lowest choice of many other voters. The preferendum penalises divisive options: those to which there is strong opposition although they may also have strong support. Virtually every other voting system is such that a majority can always enforce its will upon the rest. That is to say, if a majority of voters can agree upon which option they will co-operate to get adopted, they will have, under almost every voting system, a means of casting their votes that will ensure the result they want, no matter what other voters do. The preferendum is not such a system: a majority cannot be sure of imposing its will.

In determining a majority, each voter counts the same as any other voter. In determining an option's preferendum score, each preference that any voter has for that option over any other option counts for the same as the preference that any voter has for any option over some other. The principle can also be stated thus: as between any two options, the preferendum takes account of the strength of voters' preferences, as estimated by how many other options they rank lower than the one and higher than the other. Preferendum scores measure the level of an option's general acceptability.

Readers will have to make up their minds whether they agree with Peter Emerson in rating the preferendum the justest voting system that can be proposed. For parliamentary elections, he favours a modification of it designed to secure representation for minorities. Emerson's great hope is that everyone who reads this book will be cured of the habit of thinking that the principle of democracy is that a majority should always be able to enforce its will against any minority. Readers will learn from it how to think hard and clearly about the choice of a voting system, and come to realise the great importance of that choice. Emerson even speculates that if Yugoslavia had had a just electoral system, the horrible war that took place might never have happened: the matter is not 'technical', but of the profoundest consequence.

Michael Dummett
Oxford, May 1997

# INTRODUCTION

M any human rights are well-defined and universally enshrined. Others, however, and especially some of our democratic rights, are at best ambiguous.[1] We have the right to vote, they say, (but even Ivan Ivanovich, the poor old Soviet peasant, had that right), and that's about it! Accordingly, democratic rights need to be far more precisely stated, both those relating to decision-making, and in so far as electoral systems are concerned.

Every society is different, of course, and each must be able to develop in its own way. There is, however, the rather enigmatic position in that while nearly every 'democracy' has its own variation of an electoral system - and surely, not all of those can be fair - most use, and believe in, the one, simplistic and unfair decision-making voting process: the so-called right of majority rule, i.e., majority voting. Hence, for example, the Irish Constitution Review Group's *"Democracy works on the basis of a decision by the majority,"*[2] and Iain McLean's *"democracy [is] government by majority rule".*[3] (But hence too the constitution of the Communist Party: *"democratic centralism signifies... subordination of the minority to the majority".*[4])

Democracy, or at least democratic decision-making, has evolved into a form of majoritarianism, yet this is only a less extreme form of what was recently both its enemy and its synonym: bolshevism. Why, then, are our governments all so majoritarian, especially when other more inclusive methodologies are available? (There again, why did so many of our forebears believe in the divine right of kings?)

Times, however, are beginning to change. Scandinavia is moving towards multi-option voting. In South Africa, to quote a second example, Nelson Mandela at first rejected the old western ways: *"We did not use the majority vote,"* he once said of the negotiations leading up to the interim constitution, *"we used persuasion".*[5] How sad it is to see that their power-sharing arrangements have now broken down. Thirdly, *"Uganda is currently experimenting with a no-party state - a democratic system under which the formation of political parties is not allowed".*[6]

And majoritarianism must be questioned, if but to challenge such ghastly statements as the following, quoted at the time of the massacres in Rwanda: *"Democracy means that the Hutus must rule because they are in the majority, and the Tutsis must be suppressed because they are the minority."*[7]

## DEMOCRATIC DECISION-MAKING

Accordingly, the purpose of this book is to establish which decision-making processes and electoral systems are more democratic and which less. At the moment, a host of nations and political movements claim the label 'democratic' yet if these countries had fair systems, and if those political parties were truly fair to their electorates, whole histories might read far more peacefully than alas they do. In particular, if Yugoslavia had adopted better voting procedures in 1990, the wars which tore Croatia and Bosnia apart might well have been avoided.

In the case of Northern Ireland, we cannot be so judgmental, for the science of decision-making was dormant in 1920 when the province was established. By 1969, however, the situation had started to change, largely due to the work of a Professor Duncan Black who wasn't a politician at all but, like many another in the study of social choice, an economist.[8]

Furthermore, even in 'peaceful' countries, the introduction of a fairer democratic system would make a profound difference. In the UK, for example, if there had been a decent form of proportional representation, (PR), Margaret Thatcher would never have been prime minister; and even under her premiership, if there had been a fairer form of decision-making, the dreaded poll tax would never have been enacted.

## AN INCLUSIVE DEMOCRACY

The means by which society chooses to govern itself should be fair and just. That is, *inter alia*, any voting procedures used should allow those voting to express their 'sincerely' held opinions, (please see p 40), and therefore the count procedure should take all of these opinions into account. Most procedures currently in use are distinctly unfair; in decision-making, majority voting enables those in power at best to 'fix the question', at worst to manipulate those with less power; and in elections, the more established parties invariably support systems which give them an unfair advantage.

Admittedly some politicians talk of fairer electoral systems. Few, however, mention fairer decision-making processes. Indeed, most do not know of their existence or find them rather difficult to understand; either that or they feel it is in their party-political vested interests simply to ignore them. Sadly, too, many journalists brush the subject aside, and even some political scientists and constitutional lawyers find it a bit confusing.

This book seeks to show that the most unfair decision-making voting procedure ever invented is the majority vote, and that the best is a Borda preferendum[9] (confirmed, if need be, by a Condorcet count). Secondly, the worst electoral system in use is the first-past-the-post system, and the fairest so far devised is the quota Borda system, (QBS - first proposed in *"Voting Procedures"* by Michael Dummett in 1984), a preferendum based on a quota. These two conclusions are based on two hypothetical examples, one for decision-making processes and the other for electoral systems, and as far as I know, this is the first time such a comprehensive analysis of all the main voting procedures has been conducted with just two voting profiles, (pp 17 and 40 respectively).

With some voting profiles, various decision-making processes will give more or less the same answer(s), and this is particularly true when the subject matter is not hotly contested. In like manner, different electoral systems can sometimes give similar results, especially when a few candidates are extremely popular. If, however, a system is to be fair, it must work in all circumstances. So if a certain system does not work on any particular example, it should be discarded for something better. And if anyone finds an example of a decision taken or an election held where the Borda preferendum or QBS respectively do not work very well, I would like them to let me know. (Nothing is perfect, of course, and my own criticisms you will find in Appendices I and II, where I put first the preferendum and then QBS under the microscope.)

## NORTHERN IRELAND

In the political discussions which preceded Northern Ireland's 1996 Forum elections, the main subject of discussion was electoral systems. There were six proposals *"on the table"* (and QBS was not included). Because, however, the British government either did not know or did not want to know how to use a preferendum, they had no way of telling which if any of the six was the best compromise. It therefore did what any majoritarian government tends to do, namely, it imposed its own idea. To use Paddy Ashdown's phrase, it was *"a dog's breakfast"*.[10]

Northern Ireland needs PR, and pretty well everyone in the province accepts that. Unfortunately, however, the question of which form of PR is not so easily answered, partly because the differences between the various systems are not properly appreciated. We also need non-majoritarian decision-making, and yet, as noted in the introduction, this is a methodology which many politicians do not even begin to comprehend.

For this reason, the question of which decision-making processes and/or electoral systems are to be used is far too important to be left just to the politicians. It is actually a question of human rights.

Northern Ireland, of course, is not unique; every society deserves PR; human rights are indeed universal. Furthermore, the chosen form of PR should be unrestricted; that is, a), it should allow the individual voter to vote on a cross-community basis, i.e., to express more than one preference as in PR-STV, and b), it should take *all* the preferences cast into account, which seldom happens in STV. Secondly, the electoral system should allow the electorate as a whole a low proportionality threshold, so that small minorities may also be fairly represented.

In addition, every country needs a non-majoritarian decision-making process, one which is able to transform the democratic process from being an exclusive contest where some win and others lose, to an inclusive form of co-operation by which everyone seeks an accommodation.

## NON-MAJORITARIAN TERMINOLOGY

Such inclusive democratic structures involve some new terminology with which the reader may not yet be acquainted.

In majoritarian politics, it's 'A or B', 'for-or-against', and either you vote or you abstain; come the result, it's win or lose, and the matter is usually resolved on the basis of only two options, the *status quo* and a new proposal drawn up by the faction in power; either everyone (100%) agrees on some non-contentious issue, or the matter is put to the vote, and maybe only 50% + 1 agree.

In the Borda preferendum, the matter may be put to the vote whether or not it is contentious. In non-contentious yet sophisticated subjects, a team of *consensors* as they are called represents the subtlety of the debate in a series of options. Similarly, with any contested issue, if the question has been asked correctly, there will always be more than two options.

In both instances, after a good exchange of views by all concerned and as long as there are at least three options on the consensors' ballot paper, the matter may be put to the vote. There will then be three (or more) scores, one for each of the options, and each score will be a measure of the support enjoyed by that option from all of those voting. This measure of support is called a *level of consensus*, of which more in a moment.

## Partial Voting

In multi-option voting, a voter may cast her/his preference points on all the options/candidates listed, or on just a few of them, or again on none at all. So she may either vote fully, or vote partially, or abstain, and in all countries where voting is not compulsory, such is her prerogative. It is important to ensure, however, that a person is not penalised for voting fully, and therefore, in the Borda preferendum, certain rules apply to the partial vote which mean the value of the vote is adjusted accordingly.

If in a 6-option poll, Ms. J votes in her order of preference for all 6 options, she will exercise '6, 5, 4, 3, 2 and 1' points for those options; but if Mr. K votes for only 2 options, he will exercise only '2 and 1' points; while if Ms. L votes for only 1 option she will only exercise just 1 point. And so on.[11]

The preferendum encourages he who would otherwise abstain to vote, and she who would otherwise vote partially to vote more fully. As noted above, if Ms. L casts 6 points for her favourite option, and nothing else for any other option, that option will receive just 1 point. If it did receive 6 points while all the other options got 0, the system would be encouraging folks to vote only partially.

## Levels of Consensus

If in this same, hypothetical, six-option ballot, every voter gives option 'A' 6 points, that option will enjoy the maximum, 100% level of consensual support. At the same time, if some voters give option 'B' 5 points and others give it only 2 points, that option will enjoy a much lower level of support. But as long as the voters do not all abstain, every option will enjoy a level of consensus support of some sort!

The total number of points cast for each option is divided by the maximum possible score and expressed as a percentage. This is each option's level of consensus. In most circumstances, an option proposed in debate will be enacted only if it enjoys a certain minimum level of consensus support, and the recommended level is 75%.[12]

It is important to remember that the figure given, 'x'% level of consensus for option 'C', say, refers to the average level of enthusiasm for option 'C' amongst *every* voter. In majoritarian politics, most percentages refer to the size of the winning faction only, but in an inclusive democracy, levels of consensus, both large and small, refer to everybody.

And that, of course, embodies the two main purposes of this book: a), to identify from the range of methodologies available a democratic mechanism which may involve everybody; and b), to rectify our collective inability to define just what are the basic parameters of a true democracy. Until we do, until we define more clearly just which voting mechanisms are fair, I fear not only that the Northern Ireland troubles will drag on relentlessly with untold bickering as to just what question should be the subject of a two-option referendum, but so too, other majoritarian conflicts in Bosnia, Burundi and elsewhere, will continue to fester and boil.

## ACKNOWLEDGEMENTS

Finally, may I add a word of thanks. I have been working on this theme for 20 years now, and given the inertia which every society suffers from, it has sometimes been quite difficult to counter those who have opposed this methodology.

I could not have pursued this cause without the support of many who have helped me to run the various experiments, and an especial word of thanks in this regard goes to Mari Fitzduff and John Robb. Even more important, though, was the advice and encouragement of a small but warm circle of friends, not all of whom I can mention here, but I must just thank Alan Quilley and Ray Mullan who waded through the proofs; Jim Johnston who set this typesetter; Phil Kearney and Sieneke Hakvoort who respectively have most of the good literal and numerical ideas; Tommy Sands and Cathrine Bescond-Sands who spread the good word on an even finer note; and finally, Fionan and Moya, for he thinks, yeah, that's pretty good, and she says, boorrrr-ring.

Peter Emerson
Belfast, September, 1997

# CHAPTER 1

## DECISION-MAKING

As stated in the introduction, most 'democratic' countries use a majoritarian decision-making process. One way or another, many societies have managed to reject minority rule, the rule of the royal or civilian dictator and instead, or so it would seem, each has adopted the majority vote as the more civilised way to resolve disputes.

That historic step was actually very small, and we have not yet reached the apogee of our democratic development. Indeed, as we shall see in a moment, our use of the majority vote has led to an extraordinary state of affairs... and we will then consider what else might be rather better.

The simplest of all disputes consists of two people with two different points of view and, in such a situation, if each participant has just the one preference, no system of voting will help to resolve the matter.

So the simplest debate for our consideration involves three people with only two points of view or rather, a choice of only two points of view when it comes to the vote. And with only two points of view on the ballot paper, the only voting system which can be used is the one we have already mentioned, the most primitive ever invented, the straight and simple majority vote.

One characteristic of this procedure, even if it involves the casting vote of a chairperson, is that a decision will always be taken. Whether or not that is an advantage, in the wake of so many unwise decisions which have been acted upon over the years, in the wake of so many ethnic conflicts which have been exacerbated by such voting procedures, is at least open to question. (For an analysis of how some two-option referendums have so affected the conflicts they were designed to resolve, refer to Appendix III.)

The simplest pluralist debate, then, the theoretical minimum for any healthy democracy, also involves three people but with three different points of view, and the debate can be truly pluralist only if the subsequent voting procedure is one which allows all three points of view an equal chance of success.

## 1.1 THE BINARY METHOD

The majority vote is therefore best suited to a simple, two-option debate, to the totally polarised society where every political controversy is a choice of two mutually exclusive opposites.[1] Of such societies on this planet, there are none. And of such disputes in the world, there are few... though many are viewed in this way. Even when there are more than two options *"on the table"*, everything is still considered in a majoritarian way... for reasons which not many protagonists of majoritarianism think about let alone understand.

Let us take a simple example of a majoritarian debate, to be conducted according to the standard procedures.[2] These state that whenever a motion is proposed and an amendment to the motion is also moved, all concerned shall first debate and then take a majority vote on that amendment, for-or-against. The result, either the original motion or the motion as amended, shall be called the substantive motion. The second stage of the procedure shall be a debate and then a vote on this substantive motion, the vote again being taken on the basis of for-or-against, and either it wins or it loses.

There are therefore three possible outcomes to this debate which we will call 'A, B and C':

A    the original motion,
B    the motion amended, and
C    nothing, or the *status quo ante*.

So in theory, in pure democratic theory, there could be a pluralist debate with all three outcomes on the table simultaneously; but what actually happens is a binary process, a couple of majoritarian two-option debates-cum-decisions. The effects of using such a procedure can be very significant, as we shall now see.

Let us first assume that those participating in the debate number not 3 but 15, and of these, 4 want 'A', 6 want 'B', and 5 want 'C'; and let us also assume that all three groups believe in and use the party whip! In effect, therefore, no one group has an outright majority, but any coming together of two groups can easily achieve that numerical superiority.

In the first debate, 'A versus B', the 'A' supporters will no doubt argue passionately for 'A' and the 'B' supporters wax lyrical for 'B'; the 'C' crowd, however, who may well dislike both the motion and the amendment, might as well go for a pint! Come the vote, however, they should quickly return, for the actual outcome will depend, not so much on which way the 'A and B' people vote - we know that already - but on how the 'C' crowd cast their vote.

Similarly, in the second stage of this standard procedure, those who lost in the first vote might have little interest in the ensuing debate on the substantive... until it comes to the vote when, out of spite or whatever, they 'alone' will determine the outcome.

Our hypothetical debate comes from a remote corner of the planet called Craigavon, where it is not hard to imagine a group of four local district councillors moving the following motion:

A       That the swimming pool be open on Sundays.

Knowing that this might be controversial, a second group of six moves an amendment to insert 'after lunch', in which case it reads:

B       That the swimming pool be open after lunch on Sundays.

Meanwhile, five members of the council do not want the pool to open on the Lord's Day at all at all, so they prefer the *status quo*:

C       That the swimming pool does not open on Sundays.

The first stage, then, is a debate on the amendment, 'A versus B', and 'C's supporters are bitterly opposed to both. They don't like 'A', but with an even greater sense of loathing, nor do they like any of this 'thin-end-of-the-wedge' stuff, so evident in the amendment. In the debate, they say not a word; but come the vote they support 'A', and 'A' therefore wins by a comfortable majority of 9 votes to 6.

Hence the second stage, a debate on the substantive motion, the motion unamended, 'A versus C'. By this time, 'B's supporters are a bit peeved at having lost the first round yet, as we now know, the final decision depends on them, and they think that 'A', if passed, will cause serious problems in society and that it is probably better to keep the *status quo*, 'C'. The vote is moved, and 'C' wins by a substantial majority of 10 votes to 5.

The only people whom we have not yet described in full are 'A's supporters, and they, if there had been a 'B versus C' vote, would have voted for 'B'; better to have the centre open for part of the day, they might say, than not at all. In summary, therefore, we can represent the preferences of the three sets of councillors as shown overleaf:

| | 4 A supporters prefer | A to B | and | B to C; | |
|---|---|---|---|---|---|
| | 6 B supporters prefer | B to C | and | C to A; | and |
| | 5 C supporters prefer | C to A | and | A to B, | |

or we could write it like this

| | | Councillors | |
|---|---|---|---|
| | 4 | 6 | 5 |
| 1st pref | A | B | C |
| 2nd pref | B | C | A |
| 3rd pref | C | A | B |

Furthermore, we could depict the above democratic debate as a knock-out, with 'A versus B' playing in the first round, and the winner of that contest playing 'C' which gets a bye into the final.

$$\left.\begin{array}{c} A \\ \hline versus \\ \hline B \end{array}\right\} \left.\begin{array}{c} \\ \hline versus \\ \hline C \end{array}\right\} \underline{\qquad}$$

The final picture is as follows:

$$\left.\begin{array}{c} A \\ \hline versus \\ \hline B \end{array}\right\} \left.\begin{array}{c} A \\ \hline versus \\ \hline C \end{array}\right\} \underline{\quad C \quad}$$

Now let us look at a different but equally democratic debate, and imagine, in the same distant corner of Co. Armagh, a different *status quo*, with all sorts of frolicking going on at the local swimming pool, and on the very Sabbath to boot! Five local councillors decide to put a stop to this nonsense and move a motion which we will call '$C_1$':

$C_1$     That the swimming pool be closed on Sundays.

Well, six councillors consider this to be a rather extreme measure, so they move an amendment, to insert the phrase 'until lunchtime', and hence what we will call '$B_1$':

$B_1$     That the swimming pool remain closed until lunchtime on Sundays.

While a small group of four feel it should not be closed at all, '$A_1$':

$A_1$    That the swimming pool be opened on Sundays.

It will be obvious to all that the sense of '$A_1$' is exactly the same as that of 'A', and it is only the wording which is slightly different; similarly, '$B_1$' is the same as 'B', and '$C_1$' as 'C'. Let us further assume that in the long-established spirit of Northern Ireland intransigence, all 15 councillors have exactly the same points of view on this most serious of matters as they had in the first debate.

|  | Councillors | | |
|---|---|---|---|
|  | 4 | 6 | 5 |
| 1st  pref | $A_1$ | $B_1$ | $C_1$ |
| 2nd pref | $B_1$ | $C_1$ | $A_1$ |
| 3rd  pref | $C_1$ | $A_1$ | $B_1$ |

Again, according to the standard procedures of democratic debate, the first stage is a debate on the amendment, a trial of strength between '$B_1$ and $C_1$' with '$A_1$'s supporters gunning for '$B_1$', and so it is they, the '$A_1$' team, who this time determine the outcome.

$$\left.\begin{array}{c} \underline{C_1} \\ \text{versus} \\ \underline{B_1} \end{array}\right\} \quad \left.\begin{array}{c} \underline{\phantom{xx}} \\ \text{versus} \\ \underline{A_1} \end{array}\right\} \quad \underline{\phantom{xxx}}$$

Thus '$C_1$' is defeated by a substantial majority of 10 to 5. The debate moves to the second stage for a discussion and then a vote on the motion as amended. As we know already, '$C_1$'s supporters are very opposed to any idea of a wet liberal swim on a Sunday, and for reasons which are perhaps more connected with other political questions, they prefer to support '$A_1$' rather than '$B_1$'. At the end of the day, therefore, '$A_1$' defeats '$B_1$' by that same comfortable majority of 9 votes to 6.

$$\left.\begin{array}{c} \underline{C_1} \\ \text{versus} \\ \underline{B_1} \end{array}\right\} \quad \left.\begin{array}{c} \underline{B_1} \\ \text{versus} \\ \underline{A_1} \end{array}\right\} \quad \underline{A_1}$$

So, by reversing the order of debate, we have in effect, finished up with a completely different answer!

In other words, in any situation where no one grouping has an overall majority, the final outcome of any majoritarian debate involving three or more possible outcomes will depend upon the wording of the motion and the adopted procedure of debate; it will in fact depend upon the draw! Democracy is a lottery! Or rather, majoritarian democracy may often be a lottery.[3] (For another example of just how nonsensical is the very idea of majority voting, see Appendix IV.)

There is just one other conclusion to be drawn from an already bizarre situation, which is this: the best course of action for any 'A' supporters in such a three-way divided chamber is first to hoodwink their most bitter opponents to move the very opposite of what they want, and then hope that the third party will move an appropriate amendment!

The assumption that '$C_1$' supporters would prefer '$A_1$' to '$B_1$' could be criticised on the basis that they would actually prefer the pool to be open only half of the day rather than for all of it. In a divided society, however, those who benefit from that division often support their supposed opponents, especially when any third party is involved.

The same is true of undivided societies. Take for example the very simple UK instance of how, for years and years, both the Labour and Tory parties opposed any Liberal suggestion on PR. Only now are things beginning to change... for there's nothing like the smell of power!

There again, when the Liberals themselves were in power, many years ago, the arguments in favour of PR had already been voiced, yet they did little to change the then electoral laws, which thus still remain.

There is another example worth quoting in this regard, just to emphasise the seriousness of the question. In 1933, when Hitler was trying to gain total dominance in Germany, Stalin forbade the German communists to co-operate with their political neighbours, the socialists, and thus he helped his supposed archenemy, the fascists, to gain the required majority! The rest, as they say, is history.

## 1.2 THE PARADOX OF VOTING

After such a revelation, maybe a little more analysis is required. To re-cap on the above, we know that in effect, '$C_1$' is the same as 'C', and so too '$B_1$' is 'B' and '$A_1$' is 'A'.

Furthermore, we may recall that:

| comparing | A to B | gives A | a comfortable | majority of | 9 | votes to 6 |
| comparing | B to C | gives B | a substantial | majority of | 10 | votes to 5 |
| comparing | C to A | gives C | an overwhelming | majority of | 11 | votes to 4 |

so 'A' has a majority over 'B'... which has a majority over 'C'... which has a majority over 'A'... and it goes round and round in circles, for ever... which is why the outcome of a binary procedure may often depend upon the draw!

This phenomenon, first recognised by Le Maquis de Condorcet, is known as *'the paradox of voting'* and occurs quite frequently whenever majority voting is used on more than two options.[4] It is a bit like the 1997 "five nations" rugby internationals, I suppose, where Ireland beats Wales, Wales beats Scotland, and Scotland beats Ireland, and where nobody (but the Irish) knows which team is best.

What we have, therefore, is a shambles, a form of 'democratic' government totally incapable of embracing pluralism. Sometimes, admittedly, majoritarianism 'works'. In similar fashion, dictatorships could be benign. As a means of reconciling our differences, however, any use of the majority vote may be useless if not indeed dangerous.

Despite this fact, nearly every politician believes in and argues for the majority vote. Only the Scandinavians, it seems, have tried to devise a multi-option procedure,[5] yet even they remain largely majoritarian.

Furthermore, any tinkering with majoritarianism in weighted majority votes or other majority systems, will still suffer from the inherent defects of majoritarianism outlined above.

It is an extraordinary state of affairs, especially when the defects of majority voting were pointed out to the world as long ago as the first century AD, just after the consul Africanus Dexter had been found dead. Those accused of his murder were to be either 'A', acquitted, 'B', banished or 'C', condemned to death. And all was to be decided by a majority vote; first, 'A' versus 'B', and then the 'winner' of that vote, either 'A or B', versus 'C'. It was indeed a stark choice.

Pliny the Younger, AD 61-113, wanted 'A', and he suggested to the Roman Senate that there should be just the one vote, to compare (only the 1st preferences of) all three judgements simultaneously; i.e. , he wanted a plurality vote. He knew he was in a minority and that he would lose any 'A versus B' vote, because all the 'C' supporters would also vote for

'B'. But he also knew that both the 'B and C' teams were minorities as well, and in a simple majority or plurality vote, 'A' would have a good chance. His proposal was accepted.

The 'C' team, knowing they were smaller than the 'B' team and fearing a split vote might produce an 'A' victory, then joined up with the 'B' lot who thus won. In other words, 'A' manipulated (and improved) the voting procedure, and 'C' then voted tactically. As a result, both 'A and C' got their 2nd preference, and the accused were able to live out their days. It is not the happiest of endings perhaps, but as far as current research indicates, no further criticism of majority voting took place until the fifteenth century, when Nicholas Cusanus suggested any majority decision should always be subject to the endorsement of the minority.[6]

Later on in this book, both in decision-making and in elections, we will talk about the way all voting procedures, to greater or lesser extent, can be manipulated. We should pause for a moment, however, to discuss that other form of political horseplay, namely, manipulation of the agenda.

If there are only two options on the agenda - the *status quo* and a new proposal - with an obvious majority in favour of the latter, and if you don't like it, you could suggest an amendment thereto. Now while you might not know very much about the theory of voting, you might be fully aware of the Machiavellian approach to politics and the good old colonial policies of divide and rule. That will do fine. So, if a majority wants something which you don't want, the answer is simple: propose an idea in the form of an amendment which will split that majority.

There will now be three possibilities, as in our own example: the original motion, the motion amended, and the *status quo*. If luck is with you, the three factions - the first 'half' of the majority, the second 'half', and your own minority - will form an 'A B C', 'B C A', 'C A B' cycle as it is called; all you have to do now is to fix the agenda, and you'll get the outcome you want.

In other words, at least for as long as the political process remains majoritarian, it is vulnerable to the machinations of both the principled and the unscrupulous. Firstly, there are very few issues which can actually be reduced to a straight 'black-versus-white' contest, so it is always relatively easy to introduce an element of the grey. And secondly, any participant and most especially *"a chairperson, could, with appropriate agenda, lead the society to chose any alternative she or he most desired"*.[7]

In those debates where there are already a few amendments on the order paper, the possibilities are endless. No wonder so many political gatherings are little more than a game, as many attempts are made to fix the agenda with numerous harangues interrupted by umpteen points of order and countless filibusters. It need not be so, and this book is written from a conviction that the use of better methodologies will create a much better political ambiance.

## 1.3  A COMPARISON OF DECISION-MAKING PROCESSES

So let us now consider what other decision-making processes might be used instead, and we will then take another example of a pluralist society to demonstrate what might be the consequences of that society adopting a different democratic procedure. First, then, let us list what is available.

### SIMPLE MAJORITY OR PLURALITY VOTING
The voter casts her/his 'x' for one option only, and the winner is that option with the highest score, either an overall majority or, in a multi-option poll, perhaps only the largest minority.

### TWO-ROUND MAJORITY VOTING
There may be any number of options in the first round, but if none gets an absolute majority, i.e., at least 50% + 1, there will be a second round simple majority play-off between the two most popular options.

### ABSOLUTE/WEIGHTED MAJORITY VOTING[8]
The winning option must gain either an absolute majority of at least 50% of the valid vote, or a particular weighting such as 67% or 75%.

### CONSOCIATIONAL VOTING
The same vote is conducted in two (or more) separate constituencies - e.g., in one constituency of Catholics and another of Protestants, or one of Czechs and another of Slovaks, the two groups not necessarily geographically separated but on separate voting registers - and the winner must gain a majority in both (or all) constituencies.

### APPROVAL VOTING
The voter votes with just an 'x' for all those options of which he/she approves, and the winning option is that which is approved by a majority of the voters.

### ALTERNATIVE VOTE
Voters cast their preferences - 1, 2, 3... - for one or more options, as in PR-

STV, and the votes of the least popular option are transferred in accordance with the individual voters' wishes, until one option has an absolute majority of the votes.

## CONDORCET OR MAJORITY NUMBER

The voter is asked to list all the options on the ballot paper in her/his order of preference. Each pair of options is considered in turn, and the winning option is that which wins most if not all of these pairings. In other words, in a three-option poll, if 'A' is less popular than 'B', if 'A' is more popular than 'C', and if 'B' is more popular than 'C', then 'B' is the winner.

## BORDA COUNT, PREFERENCE SCORE OR BORDA PREFERENDUM[9]

The voter is asked to cast his/her preference points for all (or at least one or some of) the options on the ballot paper. The winning option in the Borda count is the option with the highest points total; in the more sophisticated preferendum, the answer is sometimes a composite of the two most popular options.

---

(Now some of the above decision-making processes can also be used as electoral systems, and they function in both situations in similar ways. Indeed, in the following paragraphs, I will sometimes make cross-references to an electoral system; nevertheless, may I ask the reader to remember that the topic of this first chapter is decision-making.)

Let us now see what happens when these different systems are used. Consider again that little pluralist society of Craigavon where live some unionists, a few nationalists, a mixed marriage or two and a Chinese take-away. It is, therefore, a community with all the makings of a model 'multi-multi' society, and we wish to find that decision-making process which would be most appropriate for such an heterogeneous society. The hypothetical mix is as follows: there are the same 15 councillors, all duly elected by the very fairest form of PR (for which please see the next chapter), and the entire council we will now identify:

| | |
|---|---|
| 5 unionists | Ms/rs J, K, L, M and N; |
| 6 of a mixed background | Ms/rs P, Q, R, S, T and U; and |
| 4 nationalists, | Ms/rs V, W, X and Y, |

and for ease of grammatical construction in the paragraphs which follow, we will take them as being of alternate gender.

Let us assume that after a good, pluralist debate, with everything on the table, they cast their preference votes for 5 options - 'A, B, C, D and E' - as follows, each giving 5 pts to his/her 1st preference, 4 to their next favourite, 3 to their 3rd choice, 2 to their 4th, and 1 to the option they like the least:

|        | J | K | L | M | N | P | Q | R | S | T | U | V | W | X | Y |          |
|--------|---|---|---|---|---|---|---|---|---|---|---|---|---|---|---|----------|
| 5 pts  | A | A | A | A | A | B | B | C | C | C | D | E | E | E | E | 1st pref |
| 4 pts  | D | C | C | C | D | D | D | B | B | B | D | E | D | D | B | 2nd pref |
| 3 pts  | C | B | B | B | B | A | C | E | E | E | C | C | C | D | A | 3rd pref |
| 2 pts  | B | D | D | D | E | E | E | A | A | B | B | B | B | A | D | 4th pref |
| 1 pt   | E | E | E | E | C | C | A | D | D | A | A | A | A | C | C | 5th pref |

The options could well be 'pool closes on Sundays', 'opens on Sundays for accompanied children only', 'opens after lunch on Sundays', 'opens one Sunday a month' and 'opens on Sundays'.

There again, maybe the debate concerns another important topic like the constitution. For the moment, we are only interested in establishing which methodology is most appropriate to finding the fairest result for the above councillors' voting profile, and therefore for any set of preferences on any subject.

Perhaps we should pause at this stage and ask ourselves just which option do we think is the most popular. 'A' gets the most 1st preferences, but it also gets the most 5th preferences! 'E', too, is a rather extreme option by the look of things. Feelings for 'C' and 'D' are a little mixed, it seems, but one fact is clear: some dislike but nobody hates 'B'.

And with that in mind, let us now analyse this voting profile under each of the voting systems named above.

## SIMPLE MAJORITY VOTING

In plurality/majority voting, we consider only the top row, and the scores are:

'A 5, B 2, C 3, D 1 and E 4',

<u>so 'A' is the winner</u>

with a 'majority' or rather, largest minority, of 33%. The overriding factor in this methodology is the fact that 'A' is the 'most popular' option and the fact that it is also the 'most unpopular' is apparently of no concern.

## Two-round majority voting

Under two-round majority voting, as in French presidential elections, there is a runoff between the two leading contenders, in this case 'A and E'. Of those who voted for neither 'A nor E' in the first round, Mr. P prefers 'A' while Ms/rs. Q, R, S, T and U give 'E' a higher preference, so 'E' now gets 9 to 'A's 6,

**and 'E' is the winner,**

with a majority in the second round, given the same turnout, of 60%. Again, the fact that four people gave 'E' their first preference is highly significant while the fact that another four gave it their last preference is ignored.

## Absolute majority voting

In absolute majority voting, a weighting of at least 50% is required, and with any other form of weighting - two thirds or whatever - the required majority is of course even greater. In this particular example, therefore, no one option gains the necessary majority,

**and there is no answer.**

## Weighted majority

In any weighted majority procedure, such stalemates may often occur. Furthermore, if for example a 67% weighted majority is required, any party with 34% can in effect operate a veto. In our own example,

**there is no answer.**

## Consociational voting

With consociational systems, we consider either two or three constituencies separately. Let us first take that which was proposed by the Opsahl commission,[10] the two-constituency model of unionists and nationalists. Among the former, Ms/rs J, K, L, M and N, there is an 100% majority in favour of 'A'; and among the nationalists, a similar proportion vote for 'E'; the rest of the voters, be they of mixed descent, members of other ethnic minorities or just free thinkers, are in effect disenfranchised. In this particular example, such a voting methodology leads to a stalemate, and again,

**there is no answer.**

When we consider three separate constituencies, the unionists still want 'A', the nationalists still want 'E', and the non-aligned, Ms/rs P, Q, R, S, T and U, vote 3 for 'C', 2 for 'B' and 1 for 'D', so they want 'C' with an absolute 'majority' of just 50%. Taken overall, therefore,

**there is yet again no answer.**

Not only does this system disenfranchise the *"ethnically unclean"*, it also gives the power of veto to each of the three groupings, or rather, which is even worse, to each of the majorities in those groupings. Though designed to do the very opposite, this very majoritarian system can in fact lead to the success not of the less but of the more extreme. A simple though tragic example relates to the emergence of Mate Boban who eclipsed the more moderate Stepan Kljujić as leader of the Bosnian Catholics in 1992.

## APPROVAL VOTING

Under approval voting, it is usually the punter who decides which options he/she approves of, and which not. In a recent Northern Ireland social survey,[11] a similar methodology was used in which the (hopefully benign) tellers decided, either to count the 1st and 2nd preferences, and/or to count the 1st, 2nd and 3rd preferences. In our own example, with all 1st and 2nd preferences approved, the scores are:

'A 5, B 6, C 6, D 8 and E 5',                    **so 'D' is the winner**

with a 'majority score' of 8 out of 15, or 53%. But with 1st, 2nd and 3rd preferences approved, the scores become:

'A 7, B 10, C 11, D 9 and E 8',              **so 'C' is a winner as well**

with a 'majority score' of 11 out of 15, or 73%. And there are two answers! It is an extraordinary system!

## ALTERNATIVE VOTE (AV)

Under alternative or single transferable vote we eliminate the least popular option according to the 1st count tally, in this instance 'D', and transfer its vote as Ms. U would wish (from the table on p 17), namely, to her 2nd preference, 'E'. The process is repeated in the second count, when 'B' with a score of 2 is eliminated. 'B's supporters, P and Q, expressed 2nd preferences for 'D', but 'D' we know has just been eliminated. We therefore look at the 3rd preferences, and while Mr. P's vote goes to 'A', Ms. Q's goes to 'C'. The process is continued until one option gets at least 50% + 1 of the vote, as shown overleaf.

| | 1st count | 2nd count | 3rd count | 4th count |
|---|---|---|---|---|
| A | 5 | 5 | + 1 = 6 | = 6 |
| B | 2 | 2 | - 2 = 0 | |
| C | 3 | 3 | + 1 = 4 | - 4 = 0 |
| D | 1 | - 1 = 0 | | |
| E | 4 | + 1 = 5 | = 5 | + 4 = 9 |

**so 'E' is the winner.**

As the reader may have guessed, an AV result will often coincide with that produced by a two-round majority vote, and therefore suffers from similar disadvantages.

## CONDORCET OR MAJORITY NUMBER

With Condorcet or majority number, we compare each pair of options in turn. Mr. J prefers 'A to B', as do Ms/rs. K, L, M and N, but Ms. P and Mr. Q prefer 'B to A', as too do Ms/rs. R to Y, that is, everyone else. When we compare 'A to B', therefore, we get a ratio of 5:10, so 'A' is less popular than 'B' which we denote by writing 'A < B', and in the majority number procedure in which each option gets 1 point for each pairing it wins, and $1/2$ point for any scoring draw, 'B' thus gets 1 point. (In a 'goalless' draw where 2 options both get 0, and this can happen when voters only fill in a partial ballot, there is no score for either option.) The full picture is:

| | A | B | C | D | E |
|---|---|---|---|---|---|
| A:B = 5:10, so A < B, which gives a point to | | 1 | | | |
| A:C = 8:7, so A > C, which gives a point to | 1 | | | | |
| A:D = 8:7, so A > D, which gives a point to | 1 | | | | |
| A:E = 6:9, so A < E, which gives a point to | | | | | 1 |
| B:C = 5:10, so B < C, which gives a point to | | | 1 | | |
| B:D = 9:6, so B > D, which gives a point to | | 1 | | | |
| B:E = 9:6, so B > E, which gives a point to | | 1 | | | |
| C:D = 6:9, so C < D, which gives a point to | | | | 1 | |
| C:E = 8:7, so C > E, which gives a point to | | | 1 | | |
| D:E = 9:6, so D > E, which gives a point to | | | | 1 | |
| Totals: | 2 | 3 | 2 | 2 | 1 |

**so 'B' is the winner.**

The system is sometimes very fair but not a little complicated. In this instance it gives a clear answer, but it also gives the paradox that while 'B' is the most popular with a majority number score of three wins and is therefore the winner, 'C' is more popular than 'B' by 10 > 5. So 'C' is more popular than the most popular 'B'! A paradox indeed.

The above rather verbose summary of a Condorcet count is more usually expressed in a matrix form, as follows:

|   | A | B | C | D | E | wins |
|---|---|---|---|---|---|------|
| A |   | 5 | 8 | 8 | 6 | 2 |
| B | 10 |   | 5 | 9 | 9 | 3 |
| C | 7 | 10 |   | 6 | 8 | 2 |
| D | 7 | 6 | 9 |   | 9 | 2 |
| E | 9 | 6 | 7 | 6 |   | 1 |

Reading 'A's row tells us that 'A' scores 5 against 'B', 8 against 'C', and so on, and 'B's row shows that 'B' gets 10 against 'A', and so forth. By comparing each figure with its mirror image across the (dotted) diagonal, we can see which option wins which pairing, and these are shown in tint. We then simply add up the tints to see which options get which majority number scores.

In a 5-option contest, each option competes in 4 pairings, and any option which gets that maximum score of 4 is called a Condorcet winner. Where there is no such absolute winner, as in our own example, there will often be a paradox.

## Borda preferendum

Finally, in the Borda count and Borda preferendum we add up all the points cast for each option. Referring back to that table on page 17, 'A' gets five 5s, no 4s, two 3s, three 2s and five 1s for a total of (25 + 0 + 6 + 6 + 5 =) 42; and so on. The corresponding votes table is as shown overleaf:

|   | 5 pts | 4 pts | 3 pts | 2 pts | 1 pt |
|---|---|---|---|---|---|
| A | 5 | - | 2 | 3 | 5 |
| B | 2 | 4 | 4 | 5 | - |
| C | 3 | 3 | 5 | - | 4 |
| D | 1 | 7 | 1 | 4 | 2 |
| E | 4 | 1 | 3 | 3 | 4 |

So the points table is:

|   | 5 pts | 4 pts | 3 pts | 2 pts | 1 pt | totals |
|---|---|---|---|---|---|---|
| A | 25 | - | 6 | 6 | 5 | 42 |
| B | 10 | 16 | 12 | 10 | - | 48 |
| C | 15 | 12 | 15 | - | 4 | 46 |
| D | 5 | 28 | 3 | 8 | 2 | 46 |
| E | 20 | 4 | 9 | 6 | 4 | 43 |

<u>**so again 'B' is chosen.**</u>

If all 15 councillors gave 'B' 5 points, option 'B' would get the maximum possible number of points, 15 x 5 = 75. In fact, 'B' gets 48 points, so its level of consensus is 48/75 x 100 = 64%.

The Borda count gives only the option with the highest score; the more sophisticated preferendum, however, involves the debate before and an analysis afterwards, (see Appendix VI), as well as the special rules for partial voting discussed in the introduction. A preferendum outcome will be considered a final result only if it enjoys a minimum level of consensus, and as noted earlier, the recommended figure is 75%. If the outcome fails to reach that level, as option 'B' in this instance, the consensors will examine options 'C and D', both of which share second place, to see if any aspects of these policies are mutually compatible with option 'B', the most popular option. If such is the case, they will combine these aspects to form a composite, and calculate the composite's correspondingly higher level of consensus;[12] if this is also less than 75%, they will require all concerned to resume the debate in a search for more options.

On page 1, we mentioned the fact that majoritarian democracy will always produce a decision, and we wondered if this was necessarily a good characteristic. Just for the record, I would like to recall what may well be the worst incident of its kind, a 'democratic' decision taken in

Haiti when *"the US-designed constitution was ratified by a 99.9% majority, with [just] 5% of the population participating".*[13]

The preferendum, in contrast, is not a win-or-lose decision-making process. Rather, it facilitates an accommodation. While some political debates may display the art of compromise (all too rarely, alas, in the usual majoritarian milieu), the Borda preferendum inherently encourages such an outcome. It is, if you like, the science of compromise, a logic based on the inclusive theory that all should be able to participate in the democratic process, and not just 50% + 1. There are, of course, those who criticise the preferendum; some argue for different points allocations, which needless to say could change the outcome;[14] while others question the validity of the actual options presented, and ask whether or not the inclusion of some rather obscure ones could affect the outcome. But we will come to a fuller criticism later on.

## 1.4 AN ANALYSIS

A comparison of all the outcomes is as follows:

| | |
|---|---|
| simple majority vote | A |
| two-round majority votes | E |
| absolute majority | - |
| weighted majority | - |
| consociational voting | - |
| approval voting | either D or C |
| AV | E |
| Condorcet | B |
| Borda count | B |
| Borda preferendum | B (+ C/D) |

It is fair to say that different systems are almost bound to lead to different outcomes. Some systems count only the 1st preferences; a few like AV take some of the other preferences into account but only some of them; and others like Condorcet and the preferendum consider them all. There is a quantity of information in all these preferences, so the degree of consideration is bound to have an influence on the outcome.

As it were by definition, only one answer can best represent society's wishes. In our own example, we are not yet sure what the answer should be, but because of the variety of outcomes, we can already conclude that most of the above methodologies are inadequate. Let us now therefore do a general critique of all the systems, before coming to a final conclusion.

## SIMPLE MAJORITY VOTING

In the above example, five people think 'A' is the best option, and majority voting suggests the answer should indeed be 'A'. But as we noted earlier, five other people think it is the worst! By the same logic, therefore, option 'A' should surely fail, and especially because 'A' gets no 2nd preferences at all and is obviously an uncompromising option in the opinion of many in our sample.

## TWO-ROUND MAJORITY VOTING

Option 'E' is similar: and to repeat the same earlier observation, four people think it is the best, and four the worst, yet 'E' is what we get when we use two-round voting. If it's not the one extreme, 'A' in single-round majority voting, then in two-round majority voting, it's the other, 'E'!

Because of the way these majoritarian forms of voting are counted, even a multi-option contest tends to be a battle between a limited number of favourites. If the contest is a single-round battle, there will often be only two favourites, and it could be said that the main reason why Britain has a two-party system is because most decisions are taken in a 2-option majority vote by politicians chosen on the first-past-the-post electoral system. With the emergence of the Labour Party at the beginning of the 20th century, it looked as if the old Liberal-versus-Tory two-party system was going to become a three-party affair; but because that first-past-the-post electoral system remained, and because politics always appeared to be dialectical, the arrival of a new party actually caused the demise of one of the old, and the one to go was bound to be, as it were, the piggy in the middle.

In a two-round contest, as seen in the recent 1996 Russian presidential election, there tend to be three favourites: in that instance, they were Yeltsin, Zyuganov and Lebed. As often as not, however, such systems encourage pluralism to go no further, and of the other candidates, Gorbachev got only 0.5% of the vote, which may not be a true reflection of the supposedly overwhelming popularity of the eventual winner.[15]

## WEIGHTED MAJORITY VOTING

Weighted majority voting is intended to ensure there is a fair measure of community support right across society. The trouble is, there is then the obvious danger that the required majority will not be obtained;[16] such is the case in our own example, where there is no clear outcome.

This can cause a number of tensions. As implied earlier, when there is a 75% weighting as is currently the case in the Northern Ireland Forum, any one party with 26% of the seats in effect has a veto on all such decisions. The UUP is in just such an unfair position, with power therefore far in excess of its proportional due.

## CONSOCIATIONAL VOTING

Consociational voting is another no doubt well-intentioned system but, alas, it also does not work at all well! Indeed, it contradicts its very purpose, for it tends to perpetuate the sectarian divisions in society by drawing sectarian constituency boundaries and/or using sectarian voting registers.

Secondly, it tends to disenfranchise the 'ethnically unclean', those who do not wish to be too closely associated with either one grouping or the other.

Admittedly, one can also use a three-sided version and allow for a non-aligned grouping, as has indeed happened in the Northern Ireland Talks in a methodology called *"sufficient consensus"*. This phrase was first coined (though not then precisely defined) in 1992 in South Africa for the Transitional Executive Council.[17] As in weighted majority voting, however, this methodology tends to give the veto to each of the three groupings, so making an impasse even more likely.

Thirdly, like most majoritarian systems, consociational voting tends to imply that there are only two 'main' options "on the table".

It should also be pointed out that a form of this system was used in Czechoslovakia, and the resulting stalemate in the Chamber of Nations led to the break up of that country. A majority of Czechs was in favour of retaining Czechoslovakia as one country, as too was a minority of Slovaks; and a majority of Czechs plus that minority of Slovaks might actually have added up to a majority of the Czechoslovak population, when taken as a whole. No wonder the Slovak leader, Vladimir Meciar, opposed the then president, Vaclav Havel, and the latter's proposal for a referendum.[18]

At least, in that tale, no-one died. Another three-sided version of the system was adopted in Bosnia after their first multi-party elections in 1990, and in the 18 months of the subsequent tripartite government's existence, it failed to pass a single law.[19] The system gave each of the three sides a veto; the result was war.

## Approval voting

Approval voting is rather difficult to analyse because in a five-option example, some of the voters might approve a minimum of only one option, others might approve of a few, and yet others the effective maximum of four. Secondly, in practice, people in a divided society will tend to vote only for the option they really want and the system might encourage the more bigoted sections of society to remain so. No doubt its protagonists are well intentioned, though it must be said that it was first devised as an electoral system more likely to elect the moderate candidates rather than as a decision-making process. It is, in effect, more an alternative to [majority] voting[20] rather than a sophisticated methodology.

But the idea that any 'tellers' should have the power to interpret some preferences as votes of full approval, as by implication happened in the NI survey referred to on page 19, should be anathema to any democrat.

It must also be pointed out that this system is very vulnerable. Consider what might happen if Mr. V, for example, instead of voting 'E, D, C, B, A' (on p 17) actually voted 'E, D, B, C, A'. If such were the case, the winner on the 1st, 2nd and 3rd preferences would have been 'B' and not 'C'. It is unwise to have a system so subject to the whim of whether or not a small fraction of the electorate changes its 3rd for its 4th preference.

The biggest disadvantage, however, is that the use of such a system might lead to utter confusion. In our own example, there are two answers, 'D and C', with no obvious means of deciding which must be the final winner; furthermore, as we shall see, maybe neither 'D nor C' is the fairest answer!

Given the confusion between the two, the tellers might decide to consider all 1st, 2nd, 3rd and 4th preferences, in which case the winner will be 'B', (with a majority score of 100%, whatever that means), or again, to resort just to the 1st preferences, when it will be 'A'. It is, as we said above, a most extraordinary system!

Looking at the consequences of using any of the above systems and looking back at the original voting pattern, it would seem that maybe a fairer answer is indeed one that takes the full opinions of everybody into account, certainly not just their 1st preferences, but certainly too not just their 1sts and 2nds, or even just their 1sts, 2nds and 3rds. Let us move on and consider the other more sophisticated systems.

## ALTERNATIVE VOTING

While alternative voting guarantees that the final outcome will have the support of at least 50% + 1 of the voters, it too can nevertheless produce some extraordinary results. 'A' is eliminated on the last count (on p 20), so in the end, all the 1st, 2nd and subsequent preferences of Ms/rs J, K, L, M and N count for nothing, while all the 1st preferences of Ms/rs V, W, X and Y count for something, as too do the 2nd preferences of Ms/rs R, S and T, and even the 4th preference of Ms. Q.

Alternative voting, therefore, is sometimes not a little unfair and in some instances, it also tends to function like a lottery. Consider the situation if, instead of voting 'A, C, B, D, E', Ms/rs L and M voted 'C, A, B, D, E'. If this were so, the voting pattern would be like this:

|  | J K L M N P Q R S T U V W X Y |  |
|---|---|---|
| 5 pts | A A C C A B B C C C D E E E E | 1st pref |
| 4 pts | D C A A D D D B B D E D D B B | 2nd pref |
| 3 pts | C B B B B A C E E E C C C D A | 3rd pref |
| 2 pts | B D D D E E E A A B B B B A D | 4th pref |
| 1 pt | E E E E C C A D D A A A A C C | 5th pref |

and the count, like this

|  | 1st count | 2nd count | 3rd count | 4th count |
|---|---|---|---|---|
| A | 3 | = 3 | + 1 = 4 | - 4 = 0 |
| B | 2 | = 2 | - 2 = 0 |  |
| C | 5 | = 5 | + 1 = 6 | + 2 = 8 |
| D | 1 | - 1 = 0 |  |  |
| E | 4 | + 1 = 5 | 5 | + 2 = 7 |

<u>**so 'C' would now be the winner,**</u>

with all of 'A's subsequent preferences having now been counted, and this time, 'E's ignored.

## CONDORCET OR MAJORITY NUMBER

Under Condorcet or majority number, it would seem that perhaps the most popular option is 'B'. Referring to the table on page 20, we see that 'B' is more popular than 'A', more popular than 'D' and more popular than 'E'; it is not, however, more popular than 'C'. Hence the need for the majority number methodology. Furthermore, when we examine the Condorcet results with care, we see that there are a number of paradoxes, for example:

$$A > C > B > A$$
$$A > C > E > A,$$

and
$$B > D > C > B,$$

and it would be very difficult if not impossible to say at this stage who exactly is in 2nd place; one would need to do a recount, having first removed the least popular option, option 'E' which had a majority number score of only 1, from the original voting profile. In this case, the situation is as follows:

|  | A | B | C | D |
|---|---|---|---|---|
| A:B = 5:10, so  A < B,  which gives a point to: |  | 1 |  |  |
| A:C = 8:7,  so  A > C,  which gives a point to: | 1 |  |  |  |
| A:D= 8:7,  so  A > D,  which gives a point to: | 1 |  |  |  |
| B:C = 5:10, so  B < C,  which gives a point to |  |  | 1 |  |
| B:D = 9:6,  so  B > D,  which gives a point to |  | 1 |  |  |
| C:D= 6:9,  so  C < D,  which gives a point to: |  |  |  | 1 |
| Totals: | 2 | 2 | 1 | 1 |

This means 'A' is in 2nd place. But we now have some confusion as to which option is in 3rd place, and we still have a couple of paradoxes:

$$A > C > B > A,$$

and
$$B > D > C > B.$$

Because of all these paradoxes everywhere, the Condorcet/majority number methodology is sometimes a little confusing, although the logic of its inventor was very sound indeed.

## BORDA PREFERENDUM

Finally, we must look at the Borda preferendum, a methodology which like Condorcet gives an outcome in favour of 'B', an option with admittedly only two 1st preferences, but four 2nd preferences and absolutely no bottom preferences at all! On balance, therefore, it would seem this is the fairest, the best possible outcome.

Having criticised the way the agenda of any binary debate can be manipulated (see pp 14-15), we really should add a word or two on how it is possible for a participant to fiddle a multi-option ballot: just how many and which questions are to be on the ballot paper, and can the paper be 'fixed' by the addition of another?

The answer is yes, and this applies to all forms of multi-option voting - AV, Borda, Condorcet, approval voting, plurality voting and the preferendum - for the very inclusion of another option may well change many a voter's agenda.

As far as I am aware, none of these voting procedures stipulates a particular methodology for the conduct of the debate, except that is, the preferendum. At the same time, Condorcet does not have to, for no *"irrelevant alternative"* (as such a spurious additional option is known), can affect a Condorcet winner... as long as there is one such winner.

Certainly, the preferendum is vulnerable (please see Appendix I), but if conducted according to the rules laid down, the initial debate should be able to iron out any such weaknesses. Secondly, if the votes are also subjected to a Condorcet count, and if the outcome of the preferendum - either the one outstanding option or the two or three which then form the composite - coincides with that of the Condorcet count,[21] all concerned may rest assured the final outcome is as fair as is humanly possible. If the results do not coincide, the consensors must admit their preferendum ballot paper was either inaccurate or unbalanced, and call for the debate to be resumed.

The preferendum is a particularly 'stable' decision-making methodology, and by that I mean, the outcome will not be too drastically affected by a small percentage of the electorate changing one preference for another. We saw earlier how AV and approval voting are extremely vulnerable to such minor variations. With the preferendum, however, a small percentage change in the voting profile will probably cause only a small change in the result.

The preferendum answer in our own example (p 23) is 'B (+ C/D)'. Now let us see what would happen if, as in the AV example above (p 27), instead of voting 'A, C, B, D, E', Ms/rs L and M voted 'C, A, B, D, E'.

In this case, the voting profile will again be as shown over the page:

| | J K L M N P Q R S T U V W X Y | |
|---|---|---|
| 5 pts | A A C C A B B C C C D E E E E | 1st pref |
| 4 pts | D C A A D D D B B D E D D B B | 2nd pref |
| 3 pts | C B B B B A C E E E C C C D A | 3rd pref |
| 2 pts | B D D D E E E A A B B B B A D | 4th pref |
| 1 pt | E E E E C C A D D A A A A C C | 5th pref |

So the corresponding votes table is like this:

| | 5 pts | 4 pts | 3 pts | 2 pts | 1 pt |
|---|---|---|---|---|---|
| A | 3 | 2 | 2 | 3 | 5 |
| B | 2 | 4 | 4 | 5 | - |
| C | 5 | 1 | 5 | - | 4 |
| D | 1 | 7 | 1 | 4 | 2 |
| E | 4 | 1 | 3 | 3 | 4 |

and the points table is:

| | 5 pts | 4 pts | 3 pts | 2 pts | 1 pt | Totals |
|---|---|---|---|---|---|---|
| A | 15 | 8 | 6 | 6 | 5 | 40 |
| B | 10 | 16 | 12 | 10 | - | 48 |
| C | 25 | 4 | 15 | - | 4 | 48 |
| D | 5 | 28 | 3 | 8 | 2 | 46 |
| E | 20 | 4 | 9 | 6 | 4 | 43 |

Instead of 'B (+ C/D)', the result is now 'B/C (+ D)'. A small change in the voting profile produces a small change in the result, which is as it should be.

It is, however, possible to manipulate the outcome of a preferendum, as it is in every voting procedure. To achieve a specific aim, a voter may well decide to vote tactically rather than as he/she would otherwise wish. And in the preferendum, if Mr. J, for example, decides that the compromise he fears might win is 'D', then instead of voting 'A, D, C, B, E', his sincere preferences, he may decide to vote 'A, C, B, E, D' instead, in order to minimize the points given to 'D'. Such a tactic could well backfire, though, for in so doing, he is increasing 'C, B and E's chances of success. In the case of a swimming pool, it may not matter very much; but in any debate on the constitution, for the extreme unionist to argue that more points should be given to the united Ireland option and less to the Anglo-Celtic Federation, for example, may not hold much water where the lagers are pulled in the Loyalist Club!

Voting tactically in any majoritarian debate is all too easy, and happens all the time; in any preferendum vote, however, it is altogether a little more problematic.

From the simple example discussed here, from the observations of an ever-widening circle of commentators,[22] and from a series of experiments which have been carried out in both Northern Ireland and elsewhere,[23] we may assume that majoritarianism is at best inadequate.

Yet the entire world is obsessed with this *"mystique of the majority"*, as Michael Dummett calls it,[24] and even those who accept some of the inadequacies of the simple majority vote still feel that only a better way of establishing a majority is required. Thus far, therefore, in their opinion, the democratic process remains a contest, success in which may be enjoyed by only a fraction or faction of society.

Democracy, however, is meant to be for everybody, not just a majority. The democratic process should allow everybody to influence the final outcome. Therefore, the democratic process should be non-majoritarian. It should involve a measure of give and take. It should be the means by which can be found, not the more preferred option of a majority, but the most preferred for all, i.e., that option which has the highest average preference of everybody.

The only non-majoritarian decision-making voting process currently available is the Borda preferendum and evidence would suggest it is for the moment at least, the fairest.[25]

## 1.5 THE PREFERENDUM METHODOLOGY

Just out of interest, the reader might like to refer back to that idyllic little society with its lovely little swimming pool; and if indeed their local councillors continue to think as earlier, will the preferendum help?

They voted, you remember, as shown overleaf:

| | Councillors | | |
|---|---|---|---|
| | 4 | 6 | 5 |
| 1st pref | A | B | C |
| 2nd pref | B | C | A |
| 3rd pref | C | A | B |

So a preferendum count will go like this: firstly, of the votes,

| | 3 pts | 2 pts | 1 pt |
|---|---|---|---|
| A | 4 | 5 | 6 |
| B | 6 | 4 | 5 |
| C | 5 | 6 | 4 |

and then, of the points:

| | 3 pts | 2 pts | 1 pt | Total | Level of Consensus |
|---|---|---|---|---|---|
| A | 12 | 10 | 6 | 28 | 62% |
| B | 18 | 8 | 5 | 31 | 69% |
| C | 15 | 12 | 4 | 31 | 69% |

In this situation, given what might be seen as the mutual exclusivity of the two leading options of 'B and C', half-day opening or all-day closing the swimming pool, the consensors will ask the councillors to resume the debate, to tease out a few more options - opening on only one Sunday a month, opening for children only, and so forth - to thus move to a 5-option ballot, or whatever.

Now there may be some who disagree with this methodology, for it does seem to imply that at the end of the day, a compromise can and must be found. Indeed, some may even boycott such a procedure. If, however, they do not accept a pluralist methodology, do they believe democracy is for all, or only for a majority?

And let us be fair: majoritarianism actually encourages some to boycott, as here in Northern Ireland in the 1973 border poll, as in Bosnia in their referendum on independence in 1992,[26] and so on. Turkeys, after all, do not vote for Christmas. Multi-option preferendum voting, however, encourages all to participate, either in full or at least in part.

And if there are some 'partial democrats', what effect will that have? Let us consider the situation when the 'A' party decide that they have had enough of this compromise nonsense, and that they are only going to cast their 1st preferences. The voting pattern is therefore like this:

|          | Councillors |     |     |
|----------|:-----------:|:---:|:---:|
|          | 4 | 6 | 5 |
| 1st  pref | A | B | C |
| 2nd  pref | - | C | A |
| 3rd  pref | - | A | B |

In this case, given the rules for a partial vote which were discussed in the introduction and which here mean that each of the four who vote for 'A' only exercise one point in 'A's favour, the votes table will be:

|   | 3 pts | 2 pts | 1 pt |
|---|:-----:|:-----:|:----:|
| A | - | 5 | 10 |
| B | 6 | - | 5 |
| C | 5 | 6 | - |

and then, the points:

|   | 3 pts | 2 pts | 1 pt | Total | Level of Consensus |
|---|:-----:|:-----:|:----:|:-----:|:------------------:|
| A | - | 10 | 10 | 20 | 44% |
| B | 18 | - | 5 | 23 | 51% |
| C | 15 | 12 | - | 27 | 60% |

This makes 'C' even more popular! What was a margin of 67% to 64% is now a margin of 60% to 44%, so by not participating fully in the democratic process, they actually help their opponents and make it worse for themselves.

Admittedly, 'C's overall level of consensus is now a little lower, so the obvious requirement is for yet more dialogue, and this is indeed what the consensors would demand. Nevertheless, it is still fair to conclude that the truly democratic and therefore non-majoritarian process will actually encourage the fullest possible participation. The two methodologies are worlds apart. A majoritarian system is divisive; the Borda preferendum, in contrast, is inclusive... in every sense.

## 1.6 A SECOND COMPARISON - THE PARTIAL VOTE

But now let us consider the effects of such partial voting with all the systems we have analysed. The original voting profile, you remember was like this:

|        | J | K | L | M | N | P | Q | R | S | T | U | V | W | X | Y |          |
|--------|---|---|---|---|---|---|---|---|---|---|---|---|---|---|---|----------|
| 5 pts  | A | A | A | A | A | B | B | C | C | C | D | E | E | E | E | 1st pref |
| 4 pts  | D | C | C | C | D | D | D | B | B | D | E | D | D | B | B | 2nd pref |
| 3 pts  | C | B | B | B | B | A | C | E | E | E | C | C | C | D | A | 3rd pref |
| 2 pts  | B | D | D | D | E | E | E | A | A | B | B | B | B | A | D | 4th pref |
| 1 pt   | E | E | E | E | C | C | A | D | D | A | A | A | A | C | C | 5th pref |

So let us imagine the scenario, when both the unionists and nationalists are a bunch of uncompromising ol' diehards who only vote for their own options, like this:

|         | J | K | L | M | N | P | Q | R | S | T | U | V | W | X | Y |          |
|---------|---|---|---|---|---|---|---|---|---|---|---|---|---|---|---|----------|
| (5 pts) | A | A | A | A | A | B | B | C | C | C | D | E | E | E | E | 1st pref |
| 4 pts   | - | - | - | - | - | D | D | B | B | D | E | - | - | - | - | 2nd pref |
| 3 pts   | - | - | - | - | - | A | C | E | E | E | C | - | - | - | - | 3rd pref |
| 2 pts   | - | - | - | - | - | E | E | A | A | B | B | - | - | - | - | 4th pref |
| 1 pt    | - | - | - | - | - | C | A | D | D | A | A | - | - | - | - | 5th pref |

### SIMPLE MAJORITY VOTING

With majority voting, 'A' still gets a score of 5 and...

**the answer is again 'A'.**

### TWO-ROUND MAJORITY VOTING

With two-round majority voting, 'A' and 'E' again go into the 2nd round and...

**the answer is still 'E'.**

### ABSOLUTE OR WEIGHTED MAJORITY VOTING

With absolute or weighted majority voting...

**there is still no answer.**

### CONSOCIATIONAL VOTING

With consociational voting in the two unionist and nationalist constituencies, 'A' competes with 'E' and...

**there is still no answer,**

and with the three constituencies, there is a battle not just between 'A and E' but with 'C' as well, so again...

**there is no answer.**

## APPROVAL VOTING

With 1st and 2nd preferences counted as votes of approval, the scores are:

'A 5, B 4, C 3, D 4 and E 5',

**so the answer is now a draw between 'A and E',**

while with 1st, 2nd and 3rd preferences regarded as votes of approval, the scores are:

'A 6, B 4, C 5, D 4 and E 8',

**so the answer is 'E'.**

## In ALTERNATIVE VOTE, (AV)

**the answer is still 'E'.**

## In CONDORCET OR MAJORITY NUMBER,

the scores are:

'A 2, B 2, C $1^1/_2$, D $^1/_2$ and E 4',

**so the answer is now 'E'.**

## BORDA COUNT

With the Borda count, where the rules for partial voting are not engaged, the scores are:

'A 35, B 22, C 22, D 19 and E 37',

**so the answer is now 'E'.**

## BORDA PREFERENDUM

And finally, with the preferendum and therefore with partial voting, the scores are:

'A 15, B 22, C 22, D 19, E 21',

**so the new answer is 'B/C (+ E)'.**

Let us now list these results, and compare them with those achieved on page 23 when everyone handed in the completed ballot paper.

|  | Full ballot | Partial ballot |
|---|---|---|
| simple majority vote | A | A |
| two-round majority votes | E | E |
| absolute majority | - | - |
| weighted majority | - | - |
| consociational voting | - | - |
| approval voting | either D or C | A/E |
| AV | E | E |
| Condorcet | B | E |
| Borda count | B | E |
| Borda preferendum | B (+ C/D) | B/C (+ E) |

In MAJORITY VOTING, partial voting makes no difference at all because only the 1st preferences are considered. In TWO-ROUND MAJORITY VOTING, it could have an effect, but in this instance, the answer is still the less consensual. With APPROVAL VOTING, we note a distinct change, and the system does indeed encourage the bigot to remain so, while the consensual go like lambs to the slaughter! CONDORCET also gives a worse result, but to be fair, the system is meant to be used with completed ballot papers. And the BORDA COUNT also gives a terrible result, though again to be fair, Monsieur de Borda recognised this and therefore suggested his methodology was suitable *"only for the honest"*.[27]

With partial voting, however, as in the BORDA PREFERENDUM, the methodology encourages everyone to participate fully in the democratic process. Admittedly, options 'B and C' now have only a 29% level of consensus because, with so many abstaining, there is obviously very little consensus amongst the 15 councillors. Option 'E', though, has even less, only 28%, while option 'A' has a mere 20%. As implied above, a good decision-making process should always encourage everyone to participate, and to the full. In this particular regard, the preferendum is unique.

If options 'B and C' are mutually compatible, the composite 'B/C' will have the slightly higher but still inadequate level of consensus of 50%.[28] Such can accrue only when voters co-operate, which in theory, is what democracy rather than majoritarianism is meant to be all about. And if all the 'A' supporters had in fact completed a full ballot, as we saw earlier, they would have been much closer to the winning options. If they had also moderated their stance just a little, so to persuade some of their opponents to give 'A' three points instead of one, say, their result could have been much better, and maybe they too could have gained at least a partial success in a composite. The Borda preferendum is truly a catalyst of consensus.

## 1.7 A PLURALIST DEBATE

A voting procedure should be easy to use and capable of application in any forum, be it a local community group, a citizens' jury, a school, a business, a social survey, a parliament or even the United Nations General Assembly. So let us again compare the exclusive majoritarian system with the inclusive consensual methodology.[29]

Any majoritarian system, especially the simple two-option majority vote, is almost bound to be difficult to use. On any contentious issue, the vote will be preceded by the most tortuous of arguments concerning what is to be the question, i.e., what are to be the two main options on the table. Therefore, within that debate, any new idea will immediately be seen as a threat by the protagonists of an earlier idea. Majoritarianism is an adversarial methodology, both in debate and in the vote.

Moving to a more pluralist model at least allows all ideas to be on that table. But more than that; it suggests all should allow every other party to have their legally held aspiration, and all should allow such aspirations to be debated and voted on. The outcome to every debate will either be no answer, if the participants are not yet ready for one; or it will be a compromise, in the very best sense of that word.

At the beginning of this chapter on page 7, we said *"the debate can be truly pluralist only if the subsequent voting procedure is one which allows all… points of view an equal chance of success"*. From the above analysis, it should be clear that many multi-option systems are not therefore truly pluralist. We can certainly rule out simple majority voting, two-round majority voting, weighted and consociational systems, as well as AV. And real 'parity of esteem' in decision-making voting procedures is best assured from a more sophisticated methodology, the most inclusive of which so far invented is the Borda preferendum.

# CHAPTER 2

## ELECTORAL SYSTEMS

In discussing decision-making, we saw how some voting procedures actually encourage underhand behaviour. Similarly, when it comes to elections, we may often conclude, albeit retrospectively, that everything is often conducted according to that ancient political maxim or Murphy's second law: the worst ones win. And just as, for any one voting pattern, different decision-making processes will lead to different outcomes, so too in elections, a change of system can lead to different persons getting elected. Furthermore, as we shall see, the choice of systems is quite large. Therefore, as in decision-making, not all systems can be fair, and likewise, it may be necessary for society to define more closely just what is, or at least what is not, 'democratic'.

At the moment, there are two basic categories of electoral system: majoritarian and proportional, in single and multi-member constituencies respectively, and representation hogged by one politician is obviously improved when shared by a few. In the majoritarian category (which I accept is not very well named), there are such systems as the UK's 'first-past-the-post' (which is another misnomer) and Australia's alternative vote. In the second category, there are various forms of proportional representation (PR), either one of the many PR-list systems as used in Israel, Denmark or Switzerland (where voters either choose one party, or one candidate of one party, or again one or more candidates of one or more parties, respectively) or PR-STV as in Malta and Ireland. A third category is a mixture of the two, as in Germany where elections consist of one majoritarian part plus another proportional part.

There should, however, be a fourth category, for both majoritarian and proportional systems are to greater or lesser extent adversarial and by nature, therefore, exclusive. This fourth category covers any inclusive electoral system where voters are able to express their preferences in a cross-party, cross-gender and/or cross-community way, as is the case in Switzerland and Ireland, for example, *and* where the success of any one candidate depends on the opinions of every voter, and not just on those of her/his immediate supporters. As we shall see in a moment, this does not happen with PR-STV, but does with some other methodologies.

## 2.1   A COMPARISON OF ELECTORAL SYSTEMS

To establish which systems if any actually do give a fair answer, let us consider a simple example of an electorate of 100 persons preparing to elect 4 representatives. With such a small electorate, only a limited number of systems can be considered, as set out in the following table.

| ELECTORAL SYSTEM | CONSTITUENCY/IES | | SOMETIMES KNOWN AS | EXAMPLE |
|---|---|---|---|---|
| MAJORITY VOTE | 4 | single member | communism or bolshevism | Former USSR |
| MAJORITY VOTE | 1 | four-member | block vote | |
| MAJORITY VOTE | 4 | single member | majority, plurality or first-past-the-post | UK |
| TWO-ROUND MAJORITY VOTE | 4 | single member | | Russia France[1] |
| ADDITIONAL MEMBER SYSTEM (AMS) | 2 | single member + a two member top-up | mixed member proportional (MMP) | Germany[2] |
| ALTERNATIVE VOTE (AV) | 4 | single member | STV | Australia |
| AV + TOP-UP | 2 | single member + a two-member top-up | Dempsey's proposal[3] | |
| APPROVAL VOTING | 1 | four-member | | UN[4] |
| CONDORCET | 1 | four-member | majority number | |
| PR-STV | 1 | four-member | | Ireland |
| PR-LIST | 1 | four-member | | Denmark |
| PREFERENDUM | 1 | four-member | Borda count | |
| QUOTA BORDA SYSTEM | 1 | four-member | QBS | |

Apart from the additional member system (AMS) and 'Dempsey's proposal' listed above, there are some other two-tier systems, like the German, Swedish or Maltese varieties, the first a mixture of majority (plurality) and PR-list voting, the second a combination of two forms of PR-list, and the third of PR-STV and PR-list. For reasons mathematical, we will discuss these afterwards, on page 64.

Consider, then, the 100 persons choosing four representatives from a ballot paper containing six parties - 'A, B, C, D, E and F' - each of which nominates one or more candidates to stand in each constituency, according to what it considers to be its own vested interest. Let us also assume:

+ that the voters always vote 'sincerely', i.e., that they always vote as they honestly would wish, in strict accordance with their preferences, and not from any tactical considerations;

+ that when given the choice of two candidates from the same party, 'A and $A_1$', for instance, they will give '$A_1$' the next preference to that which they give to 'A';

+ that in a two-tier or dual-vote system, they vote in both parts of the election in exactly the same way; and lastly,

+ that they have the following voting profile:

| No of voters: | 40 | 19 | 13 | 12 | 11 | 5 |
|---|---|---|---|---|---|---|
| 1st pref | A | B | C | D | E | F |
| 2nd pref | F | E | D | C | B | D |
| 3rd pref | D | F | F | F | F | A |
| 4th pref | C | C | B | B | A | E |
| 5th pref | E | A | E | E | C | C |
| 6th pref | B | D | A | A | D | B |

Before analysing what happens under the various systems listed above, it is worth pausing, even at this stage, to consider whether or not party 'A', say, deserves not just one but two of the four seats available; whether 'C or D' deserve a seat, for between them they have a good score of 1st preferences, or maybe another party is even more deserving. Do please pause and think awhile; and forgive me if I just carry on.

If you now think you know which four candidates should be elected, and/or if you want to leave all the mathematics behind and go straight to the results, you will find them and the conclusion on pages 66 and 76. Suffice at this stage to say I think the four chosen representatives should be:

'A', plus either 'B or E', plus either 'C or D', plus 'F'.

## MAJORITY VOTE (COMMUNISM)

Poor old Ivan Ivanovich had a choice of either Brezhnev or Brezhnev. If he voted *'Da'* - and there were lots of polling booths for all the *'Da'* voters - he could thus complete his service to the party and without any more ado, go back to the collective for some more socialist endeavour; but if he had the temerity to walk over to another part of the polling station and vote *'Nyet'*, in the one and only booth conspicuously placed for that purpose, a number of party cadres would approach to ask the poor dissenting Ivan just why the old hapless comrade did not like the party nominee! In our own example, only 'A' would have stood, and all the candidates for parties 'B to F' would have been put inside the Lubyanka![5]

That, of course, is all history; let us now therefore move to the present tense and consider some rather better and more contemporary systems, remembering only that the word 'majoritarianism', on translation into Russian, is indeed 'bolshevism'.

## MAJORITY VOTE (BLOCK VOTE)

If we use majority voting in just the one constituency, each party runs one candidate, and the party with a majority, or maybe only the largest minority, gains all four seats, so the answer in this instance is:

$$\underline{'A, A_1, A_2, A_3'.}$$

It is a rotten old system which nobody uses to elect a parliament, and thank God for that. But this is the way some parliaments choose their governments! Westminster is an obvious example. We have only ourselves to thank for that.

## MAJORITY VOTE (PLURALITY VOTING OR FIRST-PAST-THE-POST)

In majority voting, if each party puts forward a candidate in each constituency, the outcome will depend almost entirely upon the location of the constituency boundaries. If 25 'A' voters live in one constituency, 'A' will win that seat; and if all the 'B' voters are huddled together, 'B' will win one too. To show just how much depends upon these boundaries, let us divide the electorate of 100 into four constituencies in three different ways, Boundary Plans I, II and III. Those elected are then as follows:

| 1st preference support: | | 40 | 19 | 13 | 12 | 11 | 5 | |
|---|---|---|---|---|---|---|---|---|
| BOUNDARY PLAN | CONSTITUENCY | A | B | C | D | E | F | ELECTED |
| I | North | 25 | - | - | - | - | - | A |
| | South | - | - | 13 | 12 | - | - | C |
| | East | - | 19 | - | - | 1 | 5 | B |
| | West | 15 | - | - | - | 10 | - | A$_1$ |
| II | Left | 10 | 9 | - | - | 1 | 5 | A |
| | Right | 10 | 6 | 5 | 4 | - | - | A$_1$ |
| | Inner | 10 | - | 5 | 6 | 4 | - | A$_2$ |
| | Outer | 10 | 4 | 3 | 2 | 6 | - | A$_3$ |
| III | Town | 12 | 13 | - | - | - | - | B |
| | Village | 10 | 2 | 13 | - | - | - | C |
| | Coast | 10 | 3 | - | 12 | - | - | D |
| | Inland | 8 | 1 | - | - | 11 | 5 | E |

Accordingly, those elected are either:

| | |
|---|---|
| under Boundary Plan I | 'A, C, B A$_1$' |
| under Boundary Plan II | 'A, A$_1$, A$_2$, A$_3$' |
| under Boundary Plan III | 'B, C, D, E' |
| or, if the plan is still unknown, | '?, ?, ?, ?' |

and the only certainty is that 'F' fails to gain a seat! Given that inevitability, the 'F' party voters may well decide to vote tactically rather than sincerely, and cast their votes as per their preferences shown on page 40, for 'D or A' instead. Indeed, if the deposit is high or for whatever other reason, party 'F' may well decide it is just not worth standing at all and that, in this form of democracy, you might as well be in the Lubyanka!

In a word, therefore, majority voting may well be hopelessly unfair. There again, it might actually be sort of all right, if all the various anomalies as it were cancel each other out, and given that the English version leads to the election of both Labour and Tory candidates with even the odd Liberal, it could even be called slightly fair and somewhat proportional, a fact which I am not the first to note. On balance, though, it is a lousy system and I am certainly not the first to say that! The supposedly euphoric result of the May 1997 UK general election is as good an example as any, where Labour won only 44% of the vote, but 64% of the seats!

Some say it leads to stability in government, for at least the ruling party then has a majority... well, sometimes. Given the stability of such countries as Denmark and the Netherlands, however, that semi-bolshevik argument really does lack credibility. And what really should be questioned is the so-called ideal of a majority administration, the idea that every government can function only if it has a majority of the seats in parliament, the very thought that every controversy should be resolved by a majority vote... but we did that in the first chapter.

## Two-round majority vote

In this system, as in decision-making, any candidate getting 50% or more in the 1st round will be elected; if no-one does, the two leading candidates go into a 2nd round, in which the winner of the two will be declared elected, whether or not he/she then gets 50% (for the electorate may well now be bored). In our own example, the 1st-round results are almost identical to those under first-past-the-post. Indeed, in North, South, East and West, as well as in Town and Village, there is a 1st round winner. In the other constituencies, it goes to a 2nd-round, whereupon we refer back to the voters' original preferences, (p 40), and in Right, for example, the 2nd round is between 'A and B' and 'B' will win, while in Outer, the contest is between 'A and E', and 'E' will win.

Overall, therefore, the results may vary considerably, and those elected are either:

| | |
|---|---|
| in Boundary Plan I | '$A, C, B, A_1$' |
| in Boundary Plan II | '$A, B, A_1, E$' |
| in Boundary Plan III | '$B, C, A, A_1$' |
| or, if plans are as yet unknown, | '$?, ?, ?, ?$' |

and only 'F' can again be certain of its fate. The disadvantages of the system are similar to those of first-past-the-post, with the one small caveat: while the single-round vote tends to restrict the vote to two 'main' candidates, at least this two-round system allows up to three to have a 'fair' chance, as was the case in Russia we mentioned, on page 24.

## ADDITIONAL MEMBER SYSTEM (AMS)

AMS is a system in which every voter casts an 'x' for the candidate of her/his choice, and where every vote is counted twice. In the first count, the highest total elects one representative in a single-seat constituency, as in first-past-the-post; while in the second tally, votes are counted on a regional or national basis, and seats are awarded on a PR-list system (see page 53).

In electing two members from two single seat constituencies of 50 voters each, those elected will be either 'A and $A_1$', as in either North plus East with South plus West, or 'A and B' will be successful, as in North plus South with East plus West, or North plus West with South plus East. In any of these scenarios, the top-up will ensure that the final result is either:

$$\text{'A, } A_1, A_2, \text{ B'}$$

or

$$\text{'A, B, } A_2, A_1\text{'}$$

Similarly, under Plans II and III, all constituency pairings produce constituencies with 18, 20 or 22 'A' voters, and the result is again 'A and $A_1$', with a 'B and $A_2$' top-up. With AMS, therefore, the potential for unfair results is less than it is in 'first-past-the-post', and the only certainty in our own example is that 'F' will fail. If the Boundary Plan is unknown, therefore, the result could still be:

$$\text{'A, ?, } A_1, \text{ ?'}$$

## ALTERNATIVE VOTE (AV)

With four constituencies, again much depends on the boundaries. Let us assume, however, that every party is standing in each constituency, and that in a new Boundary Plan, each party has a quarter of its party support as described on page 40 in each constituency, a quarter, that is, taken to the nearest whole number.

The vote in each quarter constituency therefore proceeds according to the pattern opposite, with 'F' the first to be eliminated in the second count, and its vote transferred to 'D'. In the third count, 'C and E' are eliminated, and while 'C's 3 votes are transferred to 'D' (again, see p 40), 'E's 3 go to 'B'. On the fourth count, 'D' is eliminated on a score of 7, and this consists of 3 transfers from 'C', 1 transfer from 'F', and 3 'D' 1st preferences. The 3 votes from 'C' now go to their 4th preference, 'B', as too 'D's 3 originals, but the transfer from 'F' goes to its 3rd preference, 'A'. The winner at the final stage is 'B'.

|   | 1st count | 2nd count | 3rd count | 4th count |
|---|-----------|-----------|-----------|-----------|
| A | 10 | = 10 | = 10 | + 1 = 11 |
| B | 5 | = 5 | + 3 = 8 | + 6 = 14 |
| C | 3 | = 3 | - 3 = 0 | |
| D | 3 | + 1 = 4 | + 3 = 7 | - 7 = 0 |
| E | 3 | = 3 | - 3 = 0 | |
| F | 1 | - 1 = 0 | | |

Accordingly, the overall result for all four constituencies will therefore be:

new 'even' Boundary Plan $\qquad$ 'B, B$_1$, B$_2$, B$_3$'

an answer which, you might feel, is a bit of a mathematical fluke. To a certain extent, it is, but as we shall see in a moment, AV is often riddled with such quirks. In the above calculation, all of 'D's 2nd preferences have an influence on the result, and all of 'A's count for nothing; if the flow of the count is a little different, the final result can obviously be quite different too.

If the constituency break-up is not even, doubtless 'A' will win a seat or two; nevertheless, just as party 'A' might win all four constituencies in a majority vote contest in four single member constituencies, so too party 'B' may do the same with the alternative vote.

By way of illustration, it is only fair to point out what happens if the constituency boundaries are as for the first-past-the-post vote. In North, South, East, West, Town and Village, the winners are the same for the result is declared on the first count; in most of the others 'A' wins, and those elected are either:

Boundary Plan I $\qquad$ 'A, C, B, A$_1$'
Boundary Plan II $\qquad$ 'A, C, A$_1$ E'
Boundary Plan III $\qquad$ 'B, C, A, A$_1$'
or, in plans unknown, $\qquad$ '?, ?, ?, ?'

and only 'F' can again be sure of an ignominious fate.

Before we go on, let us just see how random AV can be. Take the Right constituency where in the 1st count, party 'A' has a commanding lead, while 'B, C and D' are roughly equal in second place, and 'E and F' are nowhere. In this case, 'D' is the smallest and is eliminated first, leading to the election of 'C'. If, however, 'C' were the smallest of the three, 'A' would win. Any system which relies on only some of the voters' 2nd and subsequent preferences is sometimes bound to produce unfair results, and the same can be said not only of AV+ top-up where some of the anomalies will be ironed out, but also of PR-STV, especially when there are several candidates.

## AV + TOP-UP

This is another two-part system. The vote is in two single seat constituencies of 50 voters, while the second part is a PR-list election in the larger 100 voters constituency. Again, certain anomalies will occur from oddly placed boundaries and/or an oddly divided society, (and by that I mean one that is sectarian from either a religious or a class point of view, so nearly every contemporary constituency, throughout these islands, is 'odd'). Under this system, as in AMS, such anomalies will indeed tend to be smoothed out a little, and the answer in two roughly 'even' constituencies will probably be:

$$\text{'A, A}_1\text{, A}_2\text{, B'.}$$

If, however, the Plan I constituencies are North plus South with East plus West, the answer will be 'A or C' and 'B', with a two 'A' top-up:

$$\text{'A/C, B, A}_1\text{, A}_2\text{'.}$$

In North plus West with South plus East, it will be 'A and D' plus a two 'A' top-up:

$$\text{'A, D, A}_1\text{, A}_2\text{'.}$$

While in Plan III Town plus Coast with Village plus Inland, it will be 'B and E' and two 'A's:

$$\text{'B, E, A, A}_1\text{';}$$

and so on. To summarise, the outcome will be:     $\text{'A, ?, ?, ?'.}$

The potential for odd results is considerable and furthermore, as with AMS, further variations in the results can occur depending on which PR-list top-up is used. Only 'F' can still be certain of its fate... again!

---

We now consider those systems, most of which take greater account of the voters' 2nd and subsequent preferences. Under such systems, some of the parties may consider it in their best interest to run more than one candidate, and we will look at these instances, as and when they occur.

## APPROVAL VOTING

It is always very difficult to analyse approval voting, for some voters might cast just 1 'x', while others cast 2 or 3, a few 4 or 5, and hopefully none 6, for such a vote would obviously have no effect at all. For the sake of this exercise, however, let us first add up all the 1st and 2nd preferences and count them as 'x's, in which case the scores are:

$$A = 40, B = 30, C = 25, D = 30, E = 30, F = 45$$

and the outcome is: **'F, A' and a draw between 'B, D and E'.**

So now let us add up the first three preferences, for scores of:

$$A = 45, B = 30, C = 25, D = 70, E = 30, F = 100$$

when the winners will be: **'F, D, A, and B/E'.**

The two sets of scores are very different, and it would be easy to consider other examples when the fact of whether the first two or the first three preferences are considered, would have a profound affect on the outcome. Now, however, the situation gets very complicated. If party 'A' decides to run two candidates, the voting pattern for the first three preferences will be:

| No of voters: | 40 | 19 | 13 | 12 | 11 | 5 |
|---|---|---|---|---|---|---|
| 1st pref | A | B | C | D | E | F |
| 2nd pref | $A_1$ | E | D | C | B | D |
| 3rd pref | F | F | F | F | F | A |

The result on counting the first two preferences will be:

$$A = 40, A_1 = 40, B = 30, C = 25, D = 30, E = 30 \text{ and } F = 5$$

leading to an outcome of: **'A, $A_1$, B/D/E',**

but if the first three preferences are used, the score will be:

$$A = 45, A_1 = 40, B = 30, C = 25, D = 30, E = 30 \text{ and } F = 100$$

giving an outcome of: **'F, A, $A_1$, B/D/E.**

Meanwhile, if party 'F' runs 2 candidates, the results will be: **'F, A, B/E'**

and **'F, $F_1$, A, B/D/E.**

Lastly, if both 'A and F' run two candidates, the results will be just about the same as when only 'A' runs two candidates, but if 'A' runs three candidates, the result with the first three preferences will be:

$$\text{'E, A, A}_1/\text{A}_2\text{'.}$$

In all, approval voting may produce some most extraordinary results. There are indeed better electoral systems.

## CONDORCET OR MAJORITY NUMBER

With the Condorcet or majority number system - and let us assume initially that each party nominates just the one candidate - we consider pairs of candidates in turn. If we look (on p 40) at the first couple, 'A and B', we see that 40 people prefer 'A to B', 19 prefer 'B to A', 13 + 12 + 11 also prefer 'B to A' and 5 prefer 'A to B', so the overall comparison tells us that the ratio A:B is 45:55, and 'A' is less popular than 'B' which, as in decision-making, we write like this: 'A < B'; and 'B' gets 1 point. The full comparison is as follows:

|  | A | B | C | D | E | F |
|---|---|---|---|---|---|---|
| A:B = 45:55, so  A < B, and 1 point goes to: |  | 1 |  |  |  |  |
| A:C = 56:44, so  A > C, and 1 point goes to: | 1 |  |  |  |  |  |
| A:D = 70:30, so  A > D, and 1 point goes to: | 1 |  |  |  |  |  |
| A:E = 45:55, so  A < E, and 1 point goes to: |  |  |  |  | 1 |  |
| A:F = 40:60, so  A < F, and 1 point goes to: |  |  |  |  |  | 1 |
| B:C = 30:70, so  B < C, and 1 point goes to |  |  | 1 |  |  |  |
| B:D = 30:70, so  B < D, and 1 point goes to: |  |  |  | 1 |  |  |
| B:E = 44:56, so  B < E, and 1 point goes to: |  |  |  |  | 1 |  |
| B:F = 30:70, so  B < F, and 1 point goes to: |  |  |  |  |  | 1 |
| C:D = 43:57, so  C < D, and 1 point goes to: |  |  |  | 1 |  |  |
| C:E = 65:35, so  C > E, and 1 point goes to: |  |  | 1 |  |  |  |
| C:F = 25:75, so  C < F, and 1 point goes to: |  |  |  |  |  | 1 |
| D:E = 70:30, so  D > E, and 1 point goes to: |  |  |  | 1 |  |  |
| D:F = 25:75, so  D < F, and 1 point goes to: |  |  |  |  |  | 1 |
| E:F = 30:70, so  E < F, and 1 point goes to: |  |  |  |  |  | 1 |
| so the totals are: | 2 | 1 | 2 | 3 | 2 | 5 |

We can again condense all this information  into a matrix, just as we did on page 21, and this is shown opposite:

|   | A | B | C | D | E | F | wins |
|---|---|---|---|---|---|---|------|
| A | ⋰ | 45 | 56 | 70 | 45 | 40 | 2 |
| B | 55 | ⋰ | 30 | 30 | 44 | 30 | 1 |
| C | 44 | 70 | ⋰ | 43 | 65 | 25 | 2 |
| D | 30 | 70 | 57 | ⋰ | 70 | 25 | 3 |
| E | 55 | 56 | 35 | 30 | ⋰ | 30 | 2 |
| F | 60 | 70 | 75 | 75 | 70 | ⋰ | 5 |

With a tie between 'A, C and E' for 3rd place, the winners are:

'F, D, A/C/E'.

Given that tie, we now drop the least popular candidate, 'B', and do a re-run of the Condorcet analysis to get totals of:

| A | B | C | D | E | F |
|---|---|---|---|---|---|
| 2 | - | 1 | 2 | 1 | 4 |

which means 'A' is in 3rd place but it again leaves a tie between 'C and E' for 4th place. So the answer is:          'F, D, A, C/E'

and, as in decision-making, Condorcet is a little complex. When we consider the possibility of the stronger parties running more than one candidate, however, the situation is even worse. If 'A' decides to run two candidates, the voting profile will be:

| No of voters: | 40 | 19 | 13 | 12 | 11 | 5 |
|---------------|----|----|----|----|----|---|
| 1st pref | A | B | C | D | E | F |
| 2nd pref | $A_1$ | E | D | C | B | D |
| 3rd pref | F | F | F | F | F | A |
| 4th pref | D | C | B | B | A | $A_1$ |
| 5th pref | C | A | E | E | $A_1$ | E |
| 6th pref | E | $A_1$ | A | A | C | C |
| 7th pref | B | D | $A_1$ | $A_1$ | D | B |

and the final score will be as shown overleaf:

| A | $A_1$ | B | C | D | E | F |
|---|---|---|---|---|---|---|
| 3 | 2 | 2 | 2 | 3 | 3 | 6 |

so those elected are:                                                              'F, A/D/E'

causing only a slight change which does not help 'A's fortunes at all. But if 'F' runs two candidates, the voting profile will be:

| No of voters: | 40 | 19 | 13 | 12 | 11 | 5 |
|---|---|---|---|---|---|---|
| 1st pref | A | B | C | D | E | F |
| 2nd pref | F | E | D | C | B | $F_1$ |
| 3rd pref | $F_1$ | F | F | F | F | D |
| 4th pref | D | $F_1$ | $F_1$ | $F_1$ | $F_1$ | A |
| 5th pref | C | C | B | B | A | E |
| 6th pref | E | A | E | E | C | C |
| 7th pref | B | D | A | A | D | B |

and the final score will be:

| A | B | C | D | E | F | $F_1$ |
|---|---|---|---|---|---|---|
| 2 | 1 | 2 | 3 | 2 | 6 | 5 |

so those elected are:                                                        'F, $F_1$, D, A/C/E'

which does suggest 'F' should run a 2nd candidate. We now eliminate 'B' from the equations altogether to get a new set of totals which are:

| 2 | - | 1 | 2 | 1 | 5 | 4 |
|---|---|---|---|---|---|---|

so those elected are:                                                              'F, $F_1$, A/D'.

Furthermore, if party 'F' decides to run a 3rd candidate, '$F_2$', it again will be successful, and those elected will be:

'F, $F_1$, $F_2$, D'.

This means that as an electoral system, the Condorcet method is somewhat inappropriate, unless there are certain rather strict rules as to the number of candidates any one party can run.

A further disadvantage of the Condorcet system is that it may sometimes lead to yet another paradox of voting,[6] that phenomenon we discussed in the first chapter, and this can happen rather more frequently when there are several candidates. The system can all too easily become quite unmanageable.

## PR-STV

In PR-STV, as is well known in Ireland, parties with strong 1st preference support will invariably run as many candidates as they can, without splitting the vote. If party 'A' expects a 1st preference vote of about 40 or so, it will think it has a chance of winning two seats and will therefore nominate two candidates, 'A and $A_1$'. In such a case, we must again assume the voting profile will be slightly different, just as it was on page 49:

| No of voters: | 40 | 19 | 13 | 12 | 11 | 5 |
|---|---|---|---|---|---|---|
| 1st  pref | A | B | C | D | E | F |
| 2nd  pref | $A_1$ | E | D | C | B | D |
| 3rd  pref | F | F | F | F | F | A |
| 4th  pref | D | C | B | B | A | $A_1$ |
| 5th  pref | C | A | E | E | $A_1$ | E |
| 6th  pref | E | $A_1$ | A | A | C | C |
| 7th  pref | B | D | $A_1$ | $A_1$ | D | B |

With a valid vote of 100 and 4 seats to be filled, the quota is 1 more than {the vote} divided by {the number of seats + 1}. In this instance, therefore,

$$\text{the quota} \quad = \quad \frac{100}{4+1} \quad + \quad 1 \quad = \quad 21.$$

A quota, by the way, is that part of the valid vote which ensures that any faction of a certain size gains representation. In PR-STV elections, it can be 25% + 1, and in PR-list, as low as 1%, but more of all that on page 63. Meanwhile, the count proceeds[7] *comme ci*:

| | 1st count | 2nd count | 3rd count | 4th count | 5th count |
|---|---|---|---|---|---|
| A | 40 ✓ | - 19 | | | |
| $A_1$ | 0 | + 19 = 19 | = 19 | = 19 | + 3.3  = 22.3 ✓ |
| B | 19 | = 19 | = 19 | + 11 = 30 ✓ | -  9 |
| C | 13 | = 13 | = 13 | = 13 | + 5.7  = 18.7 ✓ |
| D | 12 | = 12 | + 5 = 17 | = 17 | = 17 |
| E | 11 | = 11 | = 11 | - 11 = | - |
| F | 5 | = 5 | - 5 = - | | |
| | elect A | eliminate F | eliminate E | elect B | elect $A_1$ and elect C by default |

So those elected are:                                              **'A, B, A₁, C'.**

If 'A' runs only one candidate, however, the count will be *comme ça:*

| | 1st count | 2nd count | 3rd count | 4th count | 5th count |
|---|---|---|---|---|---|
| A | 40 ✓ | - 19 | | | |
| B | 19 | = 19 | = 19 | + 11 = 30 ✓ | - 9 |
| C | 13 | = 13 | = 13 | = 13 | + 9 = 22 ✓ |
| D | 12 | = 12 | + 3 = 15 | = 15 | = 15 |
| E | 11 | = 11 | = 11 | - 11 = - | |
| F | 5 | + 19 = 24 ✓ | - 3 | | |
| | elect A | elect F | eliminate E | elect B | elect C |

so the winners are:                                               **'A, F, B, C'.**

As was noted for AV, PR-STV can sometimes produce unfair results. It may also be criticised on a number of other fronts which, briefly, are as follows:

+ the candidate who is the 1st preference of none but the 2nd or 3rd of nearly everyone will possibly be eliminated on the 1st count, as happens here with 'F' when 'A and A₁' compete together;

+ in casting a 3rd preference for party 'F', the 40 'A/A₁' supporters may think they are giving party 'F' a measure of support but in fact, as in the first example above, their 3rd preferences may never give 'F' any support at all;

+ small parties are made to look smaller than they really are, since once eliminated, any other preferences allocated to them are never counted in their favour;

+ if a party has 20% plus support in a 4-seater constituency, it will almost certainly gain a seat; if, however, instead of five parties with about 20% there are two with 20% and four at about 15%, the question of which parties win the last two seats may well be somewhat capricious;

+ similarly, if six parties are near equal, again the outcome one way or another may in part be determined by a single voter's umpteenth preference; in a word, the system is often rather illogical and is not *monotonic*, (for an explanation of which, see Appendix V).

Its overriding advantage remains (almost) unquestionable: it guarantees proportionality to any group big enough (if, that is, the fair measure of proportionality is to be based on 1st preferences alone, but that, surely, is a contradiction in terms); STV also allows the voter the right to choose different candidates and to vote cross-party, cross-gender and cross-ethnic groupings, as they wish. In a word, it suggests the voter may be pluralist. Not many systems can make that boast.

## PR LIST

In most PR-list systems, voters indicate only their 1st preference, and parties tend to run at least as many candidates as they expect to win. The vote totals for each party can be treated in two ways: either we divide them by a set of divisors, and seats are awarded to the biggest resultant scores; or we divide their totals by a fixed quota and award seats to those parties with a full number of quotas and/or the biggest remainder(s).

There are three main divisor systems:

| | | | | | |
|---|---|---|---|---|---|
| d'Hondt | uses | 1 | 2 | 3 | 4... |
| St. Lague | uses | 1 | 3 | 5 | 7... |
| Modified St. Lague | uses | 1.4 | 3 | 5 | 7... |

A d'Hondt analysis of our example is as follows:

| Divisors | A | B | C | D | E | F |
|---|---|---|---|---|---|---|
| 1 | 40 | 19 | 13 | 12 | 11 | 5 |
| 2 | 20 | 9.5 | 6 .5 | 6 | ... | |
| 3 | 13.3 | 6 3 | ... | | | |

so seats are awarded to the scores in tint, 40 for 'A', 20 for 'A$_1$', 19 for 'B' and 13.3 for 'A$_2$',

$$\text{'A, A}_1\text{, B, A}_2\text{'.}$$

A St. Lague analysis is:

| Divisors | A | B | C | D | E | F |
|---|---|---|---|---|---|---|
| 1 | 40 | 19 | 13 | 12 | 11 | 5 |
| 3 | 13.3 | 6.3 | ... | | | |
| 5 | 8 | ... | | | | |

and seats are awarded to 40 for 'A', 19 for 'B', 13.3 for 'A$_1$' and 13 for 'C',

$$\text{'A, B, A}_1\text{, C'.}$$

Finally, a Modified St. Lague analysis is like this:

| Divisors | A | B | C | D | E | F |
|---|---|---|---|---|---|---|
| 1.4 | 28.6 | 13.6 | 9.3 | 8.6 | 7.9 | 3.6 |
| 3 | 13.3 | 6.3 | ... | | | |
| 5 | 8 | ... | | | | |

so seats are awarded to 28.6 for 'A', 13.6 for 'B', 13.3 for 'A$_1$' and 9.3 'C',

**'A, B, A$_1$, C'.**

The two main quotas are called Hare and Droop. Hare is {the valid vote}, 100, divided by {the number of seats}, 4, plus 1; in this case it is 26. The Droop quota, as in PR-STV, is {the valid vote} divided by {the number of seats plus 1}, plus 1, which equals 21. In the following table, the quotas are shown as whole numbers and any remainders are shown in brackets.

| | A 40 | B 19 | C 13 | D 12 | E 11 | F 5 |
|---|---|---|---|---|---|---|
| HARE | | | | | | |
| ÷ by 26 = | 1 + (14) | (19) | (13) | (12) | (11) | (5) |

which means seats are awarded, 1 to 'A', (19) for 'B', (14) for 'A$_1$' and (13) for 'C'.

**'A, B, A$_1$, C'**

| DROOP | | | | | | |
|---|---|---|---|---|---|---|
| ÷ by 21 = | 1 + (19) | (19) | (13) | (12) | (11) | (5) |

which means seats are awarded 1 and (19) to 'A and A$_1$', (19) for 'B' and (13) for 'C',

**'A, A$_1$, B, C'**

Another quota system, Imperiali, divides {the valid vote} by {the number of seats plus 2}, but this also gives:

**'A, A$_1$, B, C'**

Differences of course there are, and in a word, d'Hondt and Droop are biased towards the larger parties, Modified St. Lague presents a threshold to any smaller party, while Hare and St. Lague are the fairest... except, of course, that all of them work on the basis of only the 1st preferences cast!

## PREFERENDUM

In the preferendum, points are awarded to candidates on the basis of all the preference points they receive, and in our own example, the success of any one candidate depends not only on the 6s and 5s from his/her immediate supporters, but also on the other preferences of the other voters.

The full results of votes and points from the table on page 40 are as shown:

first, the votes:

|   | 6 pts | 5 pts | 4 pts | 3 pts | 2 pts | 1 pt |
|---|-------|-------|-------|-------|-------|------|
| A | 40 | - | 5 | 11 | 19 | 25 |
| B | 19 | 11 | - | 25 | - | 45 |
| C | 13 | 12 | - | 59 | 16 | - |
| D | 12 | 18 | 40 | - | - | 30 |
| E | 11 | 19 | - | 5 | 65 | - |
| F | 5 | 40 | 55 | - | - | - |

and then the points

|   | 6 pts | 5 pts | 4 pts | 3 pts | 2 pts | 1 pt | Totals |
|---|-------|-------|-------|-------|-------|------|--------|
| A | 240 | - | 20 | 33 | 38 | 25 | 356 |
| B | 114 | 55 | - | 75 | - | 45 | 289 |
| C | 78 | 60 | - | 177 | 32 | - | 347 |
| D | 72 | 90 | 160 | - | - | 30 | 352 |
| E | 66 | 95 | - | 15 | 130 | - | 306 |
| F | 30 | 200 | 220 | - | - | - | 450 |

so those elected are:

**'F, A, D, C'.**

Now if it thinks it is going to get so many points, party 'F' will undoubtedly try to run a 2nd candidate, 'F$_1$', in which case the situation again gets a little complicated. The voting profile will be as on page 50 in the Condorcet case, and we repeat it here, overleaf:

| No of voters: | 40 | 19 | 13 | 12 | 11 | 5 |
|---|---|---|---|---|---|---|
| 1st  pref | A | B | C | D | E | F |
| 2nd  pref | F | E | D | C | B | $F_1$ |
| 3rd  pref | $F_1$ | F | F | F | F | D |
| 4th  pref | D | $F_1$ | $F_1$ | $F_1$ | $F_1$ | A |
| 5th  pref | C | C | B | B | A | E |
| 6th  pref | E | A | E | E | C | C |
| 7th  pref | B | D | A | A | D | B |

first, the votes:

|  | 7 pts | 6 pts | 5 pts | 4 pts | 3 pts | 2pts | 1 pt |
|---|---|---|---|---|---|---|---|
| A | 40 | - | - | 5 | 11 | 19 | 25 |
| B | 19 | 11 | - | - | 25 | - | 45 |
| C | 13 | 12 | - | - | 59 | 16 | - |
| D | 12 | 13 | 5 | 40 | - | - | 30 |
| E | 11 | 19 | - | - | 5 | 65 | - |
| F | 5 | 40 | 55 | - | - | - | - |
| $F_1$ | - | 5 | 40 | 55 | - | - | - |

and then the points

|  | 7 pts | 6 pts | 5 pts | 4 pts | 3 pts | 2pts | 1 pt | Totals |
|---|---|---|---|---|---|---|---|---|
| A | 280 | - | - | 20 | 33 | 38 | 25 | 396 |
| B | 133 | 66 | - | - | 75 | - | 45 | 319 |
| C | 91 | 72 | - | - | 177 | 32 | - | 372 |
| D | 84 | 78 | 25 | 160 | - | - | 30 | 377 |
| E | 77 | 114 | - | - | 15 | 130 | - | 336 |
| F | 35 | 240 | 275 | - | - | - | - | 550 |
| $F_1$ | - | 30 | 200 | 220 | - | - | - | 450 |

so those elected are:

### 'F, $F_1$, A, D'.

If party 'F' is too ambitious with a field of three candidates, the 3rd runner will get only 350 points; there again, such a tactic will not cause it to lose a seat. Indeed, any party may run a second or third candidate without any risk at all, save that their supporters may not be as diligent as the party chiefs may wish. Furthermore, as in this particular example, it may not do them any good.

So back to 'F'. If the votes are more evenly distributed between all three 'F' party candidates, they might get all three candidates elected, but that is an unlikely hypothesis. After all, the success of party 'F' depends not just on the preference points of its own immediate supporters, but also on those of others. SF, for example, can sometimes tell its 'own' voters how to cast their preferences, but it certainly can't tell anybody else's!

The above tells us simply what we might already have suspected, namely, that 'F' is indeed a very popular party, and maybe it does deserve to have one or even two elected representatives. A question which was asked on page 53, is whether or not an electoral system can be truly proportional if it considers only the 1st preferences. The current example suggests the answer is again, definitely, no.

We must nevertheless acknowledge that the preferendum by itself cannot ensure proportionality, and in a bitterly polarised society - I am thinking of a land far more torn than Northern Ireland, a place like Kosova or Rwanda - the preferendum may not facilitate let alone guarantee representation to the minority.

## QUOTA BORDA SYSTEM

QBS, a combination of the Droop quota and the preferendum, can and does guarantee such proportionality. As suggested on page 52, a disadvantage of PR-STV is that it may sometimes produce quite random results. Furthermore, it may not recognise the excellent compromise candidate like 'F', especially if, as is only to be expected, party 'A' runs two candidates. While the more obvious disadvantages of the preferendum, as we noted above, are twofold: it is not necessarily proportional, and it may tempt the 'bigger' parties to run more candidates. By combining the two systems, however, we get the advantages of both and the disadvantages of neither.

Under PR-STV, we had two examples, the first showing party 'A' standing two candidates, the second with each party putting forward just the one nominee. Similarly, under the preferendum we had two examples, with party 'F' running for two seats.

We now therefore have three examples for QBS and we must look at all three. Let us start with the original voting profile shown now in a slightly different order overleaf:

| Preferences | No of voters | | | | | | Preferendum |
| --- | --- | --- | --- | --- | --- | --- | --- |
| | 40 | 5 | 19 | 11 | 13 | 12 | Points |
| 1st pref | A | F | B | E | C | D | 6 points |
| 2nd pref | F | D | E | B | D | C | 5 points |
| 3rd pref | D | A | F | F | F | F | 4 points |
| | C | E | C | A | B | B | 3 points |
| | E | C | A | C | E | E | 2 points |
| | B | B | D | D | A | A | 1 point |

The quota is again 21. Any candidate gaining the quota is elected. In the second stage, reference will be made to the preferendum scores which (from p 55) are:

'A 356, B 289, C 347, D 352, E 306, F 450'.

Candidates are now examined in pairs to see if any pair gains the quota, i.e., a pair of voters voting either 1st and 2nd preference or 2nd and 1st preference for two specific candidates. If a pair does gain the quota, the seat is awarded to the candidate with the higher preferendum score.

In this example, only 'A' qualifies at the first stage. In the second stage, there are two such pairs: 'B and E' in the darker tint have got 30, and 'C and D' in the lighter shade have 25, so the two successful candidates at this stage are 'D and E'.

With 1 seat still to be filled, we move to the third stage and examine the 1st, 2nd and 3rd preferences to see if any triplet has the quota, and there are three, shown in the dashed boxes:

| | | |
| --- | --- | --- |
| A, F and D | have 45; | but A and D have already been elected; |
| B, E and F | have 30, | but E has been elected; and |
| C, D and F | have 25, | but D has been elected. |

We therefore go to the fourth stage and identify the highest unelected preferendum score which of course belongs to 'F'.

So those elected are:

'A, E, D, F'.

In the 2nd instance where party 'A' puts forward 2 candidates, it runs like this:

| Preferences | 40 | 5 | 19 | 11 | 13 | 12 | Points | |
|---|---|---|---|---|---|---|---|---|
| 1st pref | A | F | B | E | C | D | 7 | points |
| 2nd pref | A₁ | D | E | B | D | C | 6 | points |
| 3rd pref | F | A | F | F | F | F | 5 | points |
| | D | A₁ | C | A | B | B | 4 | points |
| | C | E | A | A₁ | E | E | 3 | points |
| | E | C | A₁ | C | A | A | 2 | points |
| | B | B | D | D | A₁ | A₁ | 1 | point |

'A' gets elected in the 1st stage, 'E and D' in the 2nd stage, and while there are only two triplets in the 3rd stage - 'B, E and F' and then 'C, D and F' - each triplet includes a successful candidate, so neither lead to the election of a 4th seat. Accordingly, that again goes to the overall preferendum winner, 'F'.

**'A, E, D, F'.**

In the 3rd example, remember, party 'F' nominated a 2nd candidate:

| Preferences | 40 | 5 | 19 | 11 | 13 | 12 | Points | |
|---|---|---|---|---|---|---|---|---|
| 1st pref | A | F | B | E | C | D | 7 | points |
| 2nd pref | F | F₁ | E | B | D | C | 6 | points |
| 3rd pref | F₁ | D | F | F | F | F | 5 | points |
| | D | A | F₁ | F₁ | F₁ | F₁ | 4 | points |
| | C | E | C | A | B | B | 3 | points |
| | E | C | A | C | E | E | 2 | points |
| | B | B | D | D | A | A | 1 | point |

But the results are again the same:   **'A, E, D, F'.**

The disadvantages of QBS, if any, have yet to be identified, if but on the grounds that nobody is using it! There will be those occasions when, with a large field of candidates, the various combinations of pairs and triplets may make the count a little protracted but, with a computer and display board in the counting centre, none of these complications should prove insurmountable.

## 2.2 THE COMPARISON IN SUMMARY

Comparing all of these results we get an overall picture as shown overleaf:

| ELECTORAL SYSTEM | | RESULT | | | | | |
|---|---|---|---|---|---|---|---|
| BOUNDARY PLAN | OUTCOME | A | B | C | D | E | F |
| **COMMUNISM** | | | | | | | |
| | A  $A_1$  $A_2$  $A_3$ | 4 | - | - | - | - | - |
| **BLOCK VOTE** | | | | | | | |
| | A  $A_1$  $A_2$  $A_3$ | 4 | - | - | - | - | - |
| **MAJORITY VOTE** | | | | | | | |
| Plan I | A  C  B  $A_1$ | 2 | 1 | 1 | - | - | - |
| Plan II | A  $A_1$  $A_2$  $A_3$ | 4 | - | - | - | - | |
| Plan III | B  C  D  E | - | 1 | 1 | 1 | 1 | - |
| or | ?  ?  ?  ? | ? | ? | ? | ? | ? | - |
| **TWO-ROUND MAJORITY** | | | | | | | |
| Plan I | A  C  B  $A_1$ | 2 | 1 | 1 | - | - | - |
| Plan II | A  B  $A_1$  E | 2 | 1 | - | - | 1 | - |
| Plan III | B  C  A  $A_1$ | 2 | 1 | 1 | - | - | - |
| or | ?  ?  ?  ? | ? | ? | ? | ? | ? | - |
| **ADDITIONAL MEMBER SYSTEM (AMS)** | | | | | | | |
| Plan I | A  $A_1$/B  A  B/$A_1$ | 3 | 1 | - | - | - | - |
| or | A  ?  $A_1$  ? | 2 | ? | ? | ? | ? | - |
| **ALTERNATIVE VOTE (AV)** | | | | | | | |
| 'even' | B  $B_1$  $B_2$  $B_3$ | - | 4 | - | - | - | - |
| Plan I | A  C  B  $A_1$ | 2 | 1 | 1 | - | - | |
| Plan II | A  C  $A_1$  E | 2 | - | 1 | - | 1 | - |
| Plan III | B  C  A  $A_1$ | 2 | 1 | 1 | - | - | |
| or | ?  ?  ?  ? | ? | ? | ? | ? | ? | |
| **AV + TOP-UP** | | | | | | | |
| 'even' | A  $A_1$  $A_2$  B | 3 | 1 | - | - | - | - |
| (Plan I) | A/C  B  $A_1$  $A_1$ | 2½ | 1 | ½ | - | - | |
| (Plan I) | A  D  $A_1$  $A_2$ | 3 | - | - | 1 | - | - |
| (Plan II) | B  E  A  $A_1$ | 2 | 1 | 1 | - | - | |
| or | ?  ?  A  ? | 1 | ? | ? | ? | ? | - |

| ELECTORAL SYSTEM | OUTCOME | A | B | C | D | E | F |
|---|---|---|---|---|---|---|---|
| APPROVAL VOTING | | | | | | | |
| 2 prefs | F A B/D/E | 1 | $^2/_3$ | - | $^2/_3$ | $^2/_3$ | 1 |
| 3 prefs | F D A B/E | 1 | $^1/_2$ | - | 1 | $^1/_2$ | 1 |
| A&A₁ 2 prefs | A/A₁ B/D/E | 2 | $^2/_3$ | - | $^2/_3$ | $^2/_3$ | - |
| A&A₁ 3 prefs | F A A₁ B/D/E | 2 | $^1/_3$ | - | $^1/_3$ | $^1/_3$ | 1 |
| F & F₁ 2 prefs | F A B/E | 1 | 1 | - | - | 1 | 1 |
| F & F₁ 3 prefs | F F₁ A B/D/E | 1 | $^1/_3$ | - | $^1/_3$ | $^1/_3$ | 2 |
| A, A₁ & A₂ | F A A₁/A₂ | 3 | - | - | - | - | 1 |
| CONDORCET | | | | | | | |
| | F D A C/E | 1 | - | $^1/_2$ | 1 | $^1/_2$ | 1 |
| A & A₁ | F A/D/E | 1 | - | - | 1 | 1 | 1 |
| F & F₁ | F F₁ A/D | 1 | - | - | 1 | - | 2 |
| F, F₁ & F₂ | F F₁ F₂ D | - | - | - | 1 | - | 3 |
| PR-STV | | | | | | | |
| A & A₁ | A B A₁ C | 2 | 1 | 1 | - | - | - |
| | A F B C | 1 | 1 | 1 | - | - | 1 |
| PR-list | | | | | | | |
| d'Hondt | A A₁ B A₂ | 3 | 1 | - | - | - | - |
| St Lague | A B A₁ C | 2 | 1 | 1 | - | - | - |
| mod St Lague | A B A₁ C | 2 | 1 | 1 | - | - | - |
| Hare | A B A₁ C | 2 | 1 | 1 | - | - | - |
| Droop | A A₁ B C | 2 | 1 | 1 | - | - | - |
| Imperiali | A A₁ B C | 2 | 1 | 1 | - | - | - |
| PREFERENDUM | | | | | | | |
| | F A D C | 1 | - | 1 | 1 | - | 1 |
| F & F₁ | F F₁ A D | 1 | - | - | 1 | - | 2 |
| QUOTA BORDA SYSTEM (QBS) | | | | | | | |
| | A E D F | 1 | - | - | 1 | 1 | 1 |
| A & A₁ or F & F₁ | A E D F | 1 | - | - | 1 | 1 | 1 |

## 2.3 A YUGOSLAV REFLECTION

Nearly every system gives a different answer, yet nearly all are called democratic!

Before proceeding further with this analysis, we must remember that the practical consequences of using only 'semi-democratic' systems can often be tragic. *"Croatia's British first-past-the-post, single-member-constituency electoral system gave Tudjman's party an absolute majority of the seats, even though it had won fewer than half of the votes;"*[8] while *"Milošević took a leaf out of the British electoral book and [designed] a system whereby he would still enjoy absolute political control with less than 50% of the vote."*[9]

Meanwhile, in the Bosnian elections of 1990, the one moderate candidate who might have been able to save that land from a descent into war - Ante Marković - was probably the 2nd or 3rd preference of almost everybody. He lost, gaining only 13 of 240 seats. In all probability, PR-STV would not have saved him. Known affectionately as the last Yugoslav, he retired shortly afterwards. The winners in that election were the three nationalist parties which *"had secretly agreed before the elections to form a coalition government"*[10] but, having thus got rid of the moderates, they then argued amongst themselves, like rotten thieves... well, two rotten thieves, Boban and Karadžić, and one uncertain other, Izetbegović.[11]

## 2.4 ANALYSIS

Looking at our own example, there were bound to be differences between the results of all the various systems. After all, as in decision-making, some of them take only the 1st preferences into account; a few like PR-STV consider some of the voters' other preferences, but only some of them; and only three systems, Condorcet, the preferendum and QBS take note of all the preferences cast by everybody.

Furthermore, while Condorcet gives a result which is that candidate who enjoys an absolute majority, both the preferendum and QBS are electoral systems which are more inclusive. In other words, in either of the latter two systems, the success of any one candidate does not depend solely on the votes of a certain percentage of the electorate, namely, his/her immediate supporters; (and that certain percentage may be a majority, the largest minority or, as in PR, a minimum proportion). Rather, as in preferendum decision-making, any success depends on the preference points of everybody who votes.

If a system is to be truly proportional, it must not be restrictive; in other words, it must allow if not encourage the voter to list at least some preferences, and to do that properly, it must take these other preferences into account. Of the systems mentioned, the preferendum, QBS, PR-STV, a form of list system used in Luxembourg and Switzerland, of which more in a moment, and AV have this quality, but very much in descending order.

Furthermore, we must accept that there are degrees of proportionality. In a PR-STV election of three representatives, any candidate with a quota of 25% + 1 of the 1st preference vote is bound to get elected, for even if there are only four candidates, and if the first three each get 25% + 1, the fourth can only possibly get a maximum of 25% - 3, and will therefore lose. Such a PR election is therefore said to have a threshold of 25%.

In similar fashion, a PR-STV election in a four-seater has a threshold of 20%, which still makes life quite difficult for a party with only 10% support. And in fact, given that PR-STV is rarely used in anything bigger than a 6- or 7-seater (for otherwise the counts could become absolute marathons), such parties may always remain in the cold.

With PR-list systems, however, the constituency can be as big as you like. In a 20-seater, the threshold is down to 5%; in a 100-seater, needless to say, it is 1%; and in The Netherlands[12], where the entire country forms just the one constituency for all 150 members of their parliament, the threshold is 0.67%.

Brilliant, the small party might say. As noted earlier, however, PR-list works only on 1st preferences, with just those two exceptions, the list systems we referred to in Luxembourg and Switzerland, and the latter for example, allows the voter to vote for as many candidates as there are seats to be awarded, and it is therefore used in fairly small constituencies with a relatively high threshold.

In most other list systems, the voter chooses just one candidate from one party, and he/she is not able to vote for any other candidates let alone any other party.

And in the worst sort of list system ever concocted, as used often in Israel, just the once in Northern Ireland[13] in May 1996, and once so far in South Africa, in their first multi-party elections in 1994, the punter is allowed to identify only the party of her/his choice. In consequence, all power of candidate selection is given to the party political machine. Brezhnev would have liked that.

In our own example, the very popular 'F' gets only 5 of the 1st preference votes, and so the Dutch system would have given 'F' just 5% of the seats. Better than nothing, you might say, which is what 'F' would definitely get in the UK, and probably get in Ireland. But at least the PR-list system allows the voter to vote sincerely rather than tactically.

Now quite unlike PR-STV which gives a healthy choice to the voter, (it is the counting mechanism of PR-STV which is not so good), PR-list gives far too much political power to the party political machine and far too little chance to any independent candidate. Secondly, in the Dutch scenario, there is the off-chance that all the candidates elected will come from, say, Amsterdam, and any sense of local representation may perhaps be lost when the constituency is too large.

For this reason, certain countries have had the good sense to use a two-tier system: Sweden, Germany and Malta were the ones we mentioned. In the Swedish model, the first PR-list election is in small constituencies, and the second PR-list count is in either a few regional, or just the one national, constituency(ies). So they get the best of two worlds: local representation and fair (1st preference) proportionality.

(This two-tier system was not included in our own example, for the number of seats to be awarded was only 4, and 4 either splits into two identical 2-seater constituencies as opposed to some small and one large one, or you get three 1-seaters and one 3-seater, but a l-seater, of course, cannot be proportional.)

Most of these two-tier systems use two variations of PR list, and the result is often pretty good. One system is worse, the German model, for it uses the single-seat majority or plurality vote in the first tier; and one is better, for Malta combines PR-STV, which has its excellent local identity and cross-party voting characteristics, with the equally excellent PR-list to ensure overall (1st preference) proportionality. Accordingly, those little islanders get the best of three worlds: local representation, fair proportionality and voters' pluralism.

None, however, has the best of all worlds; yet a combination of QBS with a PR-list (preferendum type of) top-up based on some if not all preferences cast would seem to be ideal.[14]

Certainly, looking back at the above example, it is possible to say which four persons should probably be elected. Candidate 'A' with 40 in number

1st preferences, is a keen contender; either 'B or E' is another, and of the 30 persons who gave their 1st/2nd preferences to 'B and E', none will be happy if only 'A' gets elected; in similar fashion, either 'C or D' deserves representation, and it is probably fair to say that it does not matter very much *to the electorate* which of the two actually wins the election; what is true, however, is that 'C and D' supporters also don't like party 'A' very much. Finally, there is 'F', and while 'F' as we noted earlier is the 1st preference of only five voters, it is the 2nd or 3rd preference of literally everybody else, all 95 of them and obviously, therefore, deserves at least one seat. In theory, then, as we hinted on page 41, the winning candidates should be:

| | |
|---|---|
| Either | A |
| and maybe another | $A_1$ |
| plus either | B or E |
| plus either | C or D |
| plus | F |
| and maybe another | $F_1$ |

Given, however, that while 'A' does get 40 first preferences, it gets no seconds and only 5 thirds, and some 40+ voters give 'A' only a 5th or 6th preference, we may safely say that, proportionately, 'A' deserves only one success. In similar fashion, if 'F' is going to get a 2nd representative, then either 'A' voters, or 'B and E' voters, or again 'C and D' voters will lose, and that too would be unfair. The final answer should therefore be:

'A, plus either B or E, plus either C or D, plus F'.

In other words, a fair result would be:

| | |
|---|---|
| either | A  B  C  F |
| or | A  B  D  F |
| or | A  C  E  F |
| or | A  D  E  F |

Well, Leonid Brezhnev for one would be disappointed to learn that communism wasn't really a democratic electoral system. Equally, however, many other political leaders, past and present - people like Bill Clinton, Margaret Thatcher, Tony Blair and Slobodan Milošević[15] - may well be reluctant to accept that they were also elected into office by electoral systems which are not very democratic. In our own example, the only electoral systems which qualify as fair are:

| QBS | | | | | A | B | C | D | E | F |
|---|---|---|---|---|---|---|---|---|---|---|
| | A | E | D | F | 1 | - | - | 1 | 1 | 1 |
| APPROVAL VOTING | | | | | | | | | | |
| 2 prefs | F | A | B/E/D | | 1 | 2/3 | - | 2/3 | 2/3 | 1 |
| 3 prefs | F | D | A | B/E | 1 | 1/2 | - | 1 | 1/2 | 1 |
| CONDORCET | | | | | | | | | | |
| A & A₁ | F | A/D/E | | | 1 | - | - | 1 | 1 | 1 |
| PR-STV | | | | | | | | | | |
| | A | F | B | C | 1 | 1 | 1 | - | - | 1 |

PR-STV and approval voting are in tint because they give these fair answers only if parties 'A' and 'A and F' do not stand two candidates, but there is nothing in the rules of these electoral systems to stop them so doing. And Condorcet is hatched because it gives a fair outcome only when 'A' has two candidates, but if 'A' is to run two, 'F' will want to run two as well, which as we saw (on p 50) produces a most unfair result.

(We should point out that the protagonists of Condorcet promote this methodology for decision-making rather than as an electoral system, and when seeking a decision, of course, only one answer is possible; neither party 'F' nor anyone else for that matter would want to propose more than one option.) So QBS, it would seem, is the only system which produces a fair outcome.

The 100 citizens voted for only four representatives and, as we mentioned earlier, it was therefore rather difficult to consider any two-tier systems. If, however, thousands or millions elect a house of dozens or an hundred odd, all sorts of two-tier or top-up arrangements are possible, and just to summarise, these include:

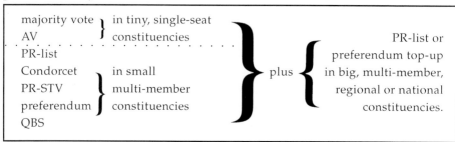

majority vote ⎫ in tiny, single-seat
AV ⎭ constituencies

PR-list
Condorcet ⎫ in small
PR-STV ⎬ multi-member
preferendum ⎭ constituencies
QBS

⎫ plus ⎧ PR-list or
⎬ ⎨ preferendum top-up in big, multi-member, regional or national constituencies.

Some of these, like PR-STV plus a top-up, approach perfection, but the main conclusion from this paper is that the best would be QBS + a (preferendum based) top-up. Furthermore, such a system is appropriate for Northern Ireland and England, and the Republic of Ireland, and Bosnia, and Rwanda, and so on. It must be thus. If any democratic instrument is relevant to only those lands which are not in conflict, it must be dismissed as too dangerous.

## 2.5 QBS + a Preferendum Top-up

The best houses are built not only of glass, or wood, or brick; but once built, they are easy to live in... in theory! In similar fashion, the best electoral system for any 'multi-multi' society is almost bound to be a little complex to count (and very easy to use)... but in this the age of the computer, the actual calculations need not be a serious problem.

*Ipso facto*, the complete opposite, a rotten system is probably quite difficult to use and dead easy to understand. The British first-past-the-post says it all. The first complication is the question of where to draw the constituency boundaries? The process is protracted and the arguments at least unnecessary, yet such are the inevitable consequences of using any simple majoritarian system such as first-past-the-post and AV, and to a lesser extent their cousins, AMS and AV + top-up. Similarly in PR-STV, as the Irish will tell you, there are arguments a'plenty over the constituency boundaries, as parties with 50% local support try to turn a 3-seater into a 4-seater but not a 5-seater, while those with 40% argue for either the 3- or a 5-seater.

The second complication of the British system relates to what is, for some, a truly vexed question: how on earth is the poor punter going to vote in a constituency of three or four near-equal contenders, where the winner (sic) may be the candidate who respectively, 66% or 74% do not vote for!? Many an Englander is confronted by this three-horse dilemma where Lib., Lab. and Tory fight it out; and many a Scot is faced by a quadruple choice, as the SNP joins in the fray. Counting a first-past-the-post election, oh yes, that is absolute child's play.

An electoral system of QBS + a preferendum based top-up sounds pretty complicated, but this is mainly because the terminology is relatively new. On closer examination, it is in fact very easy to use, for the voter merely casts her/his preference points for (one, some or hopefully) all the candidates listed. And given the fact that the preferendum, as we saw in the last chapter, is rather difficult to manipulate, it is probably far easier to use than so many other systems which tempt the voter to vote tactically rather than sincerely.

It is certainly easier to apply, for with a top-up - and especially a top-up based not on 1st preferences alone but on something like the preferendum scores - any debate over the location of the constituency boundaries is more likely to be a discussion and not an argument, for any loss on a boundary swing may well be a gain on the top-up roundabout.

Finally, it is fairly easy to count, for all we have to do is to add up the points and look at the quota; as we said earlier, there are none of the PR-STV complications of surpluses and eliminations and transfers of fractious factions.

## 2.6 A SECOND COMPARISON - THE PARTIAL VOTE

Before reaching a definite conclusion, we should also consider what happens if some use only a partial vote, just as we did in the first chapter. Let us now therefore consider the case when the 40 'A' supporters along with their most bitter opponents, the 25 'C/D' supporters, vote for only their 1st and 1st/2nd preferences respectively, like this:

| No of voters | 40 | 19 | 13 | 12 | 11 | 5 |
|---|---|---|---|---|---|---|
| 1st  pref | A | B | C | D | E | F |
| 2nd  pref | - | E | D | C | B | D |
| 3rd  pref | - | F | - | - | F | A |
| 4th  pref | - | C | - | - | A | E |
| 5th  pref | - | A | - | - | C | C |
| 6th  pref | - | D | - | - | D | B |

### MAJORITY VOTE (COMMUNISM, BLOCK VOTE AND FIRST-PAST-THE-POST)

Under communism, the bolsheviks still win. That goes without saying. The same is true of the block vote. So, too, with majority voting, everything still depends on only the 1st preferences, so the results still depend mainly on the whereabouts of the constituency boundaries.

### TWO-ROUND MAJORITY VOTE

Again, in two-round voting, much still depends on the lie of the constituencies, though here we see a little variation and the outcome in Outer of Boundary Plan II, for example, is a draw between 'A and E'; cf. page 43.

## AMS and AV

In AMS and AV, the results are much the same as before, but in AV, if every constituency is identical, the answer will now be a victory for 'A'.

## AV + TOP-UP

AV + top-up, however, leads to some changes. In Town plus Coast with Village plus Inland, the result is now 'A and $A_1$', plus a 'B and $A_2$' top-up, while in Town plus Inland with Village plus Coast, the answer is an 'A/ B' draw and 'C', plus an '$A_1$ and $A_2$' top-up. If this is your system, it pays to be a bigot!

## PR-LIST

Indeed, all such unsophisticated majoritarian systems tend to persuade the intransigent to remain unmoved and uncompromising; similarly, because most PR-list systems allow the voter only one preference, they too are unaffected by any partial voting. So let us move on.

## APPROVAL VOTING

In approval voting, on a count of just the 1st and 2nd preferences cast, 'A, B, D and E' get in, and poor old 'F' is left out. When the first three preferences are counted, however, 'F' is once again successful. It is still, therefore, very difficult to analyse; and it would still encourage the intransigent 'A' party to stand more than one candidate, that or split into two sister parties, to achieve the same result.

---

Obviously the main changes occur with those systems which consider all preferences. Some of the outcomes are listed below, and if any party does well when all parties run just the one candidate, it will sometimes be even more successful if it runs two or three. The full set of relevant results is listed on page 71.

## CONDORCET

In Condorcet, for example, the score now becomes:

$$'A = 5, B = 3, C = 1^1/_2, D = 1, E = 2^1/_2 \text{ and } F = 2',$$

so those elected are:                                                    **'A, B, E, F',**

while if 'A' runs two candidates, they are:                    **'A, $A_1$, B, E/F'.**

## PR-STV

With parties running one candidate, the winners are: **'A, B, C, D',**

but with party 'A' running two candidates, the winners are:

**'A, B, A$_1$, C'.**

## BORDA COUNT

In the Borda count system with all parties running just the one candidate, the scores are:

'A = 331, B = 174, C = 227, D = 192, E = 176 and F = 150',

so those elected are: **'A, C, D, E',**

but if both 'A and A$_1$' run, those elected will be **'A, A$_1$, C, D'.**

## PREFERENDUM

With the preferendum, the partial vote rule comes into play and the scores are:

'A = 131, B = 174, C = 127, D = 92, E = 176, and F = 150',

so those elected are **'E, B, F, A',**

while if both 'F and F$_1$' run the winners are: **'E, B, F, F$_1$.'**

## QBS

QBS may be based, either on a Borda count without the partial vote rule, or on the preferendum which does use that rule.[16] We must now, therefore, make that distinction.

## QBS (BORDA)

In this instance, the scores are: **'A, E, C, D'.**

but when 'A' runs two candidates, the winners will be: **'A, E, C, A$_1$'.**

## QBS (PREFERENDUM)

With all parties running just the one candidate, those elected are:

**'B, F, E, A'.**

Let us now compare these findings with the results we obtained when the punters all completed a full ballot paper. We saw how both the majoritarian and the PR-list systems vary either a little or not at all in partial voting, the exception being AV + top-up in certain constituencies, though any changes in that only give 'A' an even greater advantage. As far as the more sophisticated methodologies are concerned, a comparison leads to the following table:

| | Full ballot | Partial ballot |
|---|---|---|
| CONDORCET | | |
| | F  D  A  C | A   B  E/F |
| A & A$_1$ | F     A/D/E | A  A$_1$  B  E/F |
| F & F$_1$ | F  F$_1$  D  A | A   B  E/F |
| F, F$_1$ & F$_2$ | F  F$_1$  F$_2$  D | A   B  E/F |
| | | |
| PR-STV | | |
| | A  F  B  C | A  B  C  D |
| A & A$_1$ | A  B  A$_1$  C | A  B  A$_1$  C |
| | | |
| BORDA | | |
| | F  A  D  C | A  C  D  E |
| A & A$_1$ | F  A  D  E | A  A$_1$  C  D |
| F & F$_1$ | F  F$_1$  A  D | A  C  E  B |
| | | |
| PREFERENDUM | | |
| | F  A  D  C | E  B  F  A |
| F & F$_1$ | F  F$_1$  A  D | E  B  F  F$_1$ |
| B & B$_1$ | F  A  D  C | B  E  B$_1$  F |
| E & E$_1$ | F  A  D  C | E  B  E$_1$  F |
| | | |
| QBS (BORDA) | | |
| | A  E  D  F | A  E  C  D |
| A & A$_1$ | A  E  D  F | A  E  C  A$_1$ |
| | | |
| QBS (PREFERENDUM) | | |
| | A  E  D  F | B  E  F  A |
| A & A$_1$ | A  E  C  F | B  E  A  F |
| F & F$_1$ | A  E  D  F | B  E  F  F$_1$ |
| B & B$_1$ | A  D  E  F | B  E  B$_1$  F |
| E & E$_1$ | A  D  E  F | B  E  E$_1$  F |

We decided earlier that when everyone hands in a completed ballot paper, a fair result would be:

| either | A B C F |
|--------|---------|
| or | A B D F |
| or | A C E F |
| or | A D E F |

which led us to the conclusion that the only electoral system which qualifies as fair is QBS.

In the partial vote scenario, it is rather more difficult to say just exactly what is fair, for we cannot now know for sure how 65 voters regard some of the other candidates, yet regard they surely must. The DUP voter, for example, even though he only votes DUP 1, 2 and 3, presumably agrees with his colleagues in the Loyalist Club that the UUP nominee is nevertheless better than the SF candidate. (Judging by the pre-election rhetoric, it is sometimes difficult to know; by the post-election verbiage, it is often even more difficult!) We cannot know for certain, therefore, just what a fair result should be, though we can say it should be at least as before, with if anything a bias towards 'B, E and/or F', the three parties whose supporters continue to express all their preferences.

In fact, as we can see from the comparison, the actual results are often the other way around, and a number of electoral systems, shown here in hatched, actually benefit those who vote only partially.

Of the unhatched methodologies, those results which appear to be fair, whether or not the punters hand in full or partial ballots, are:

+ Condorcet and the preferendum, when they allow parties to field only the one candidate; and

+ QBS (preferendum).

Now most politicians are really quite devious, and where rules state that only one party can stand, those concerned may well split their party into two, which rather suggests Condorcet and the preferendum might not be suitable.

On the other hand, most voters are really quite clever,[17] and most vote in their own best interest, adjusting their vote if need be to the particular system in use. If QBS (preferendum) were indeed in use, most voters would probably fill in a pretty full ballot paper and, mindful of the quota, parties would not want to nominate too many candidates. As has been said elsewhere, a good system is one which is difficult to manipulate; besides its many other attributes, QBS is exactly that!

## 2.7 THE DEMOCRATIC IDEAL

From the analysis of this chapter, a fair electoral system may be defined as one which is inclusive and proportional. To be inclusive, the voter must be able to vote in her/his own order of preference for more than one candidate of more than one party; furthermore, all these preferences must bear an influence on the final result. And to be proportional, an electoral system must allow minorities to be fairly represented, i.e., in a manner which takes account of more than just the voters' first preferences.

I look forward to the day when an international tribunal decides that first-past-the-post voting is an infringement of that electorate's human rights; that proportionality is a prerequisite of any electoral system and that a true proportionality must be based on a pluralist electoral system which not only allows (as in AV) but actually encourages (cf. the preferendum) the voter to exercise a number of preferences, cross-candidate, cross-gender and cross-party. In all, I long for the two-tier QBS preferendum + top-up to be laid down as the most democratic system, at least until such time as someone else invents something even fairer.

With such ideas in mind, we might also dream of the day when the principle of proportionality is accepted not only for parliament but also for government, which brings us to a QBS matrix vote[18] and a most inclusive form of power-sharing. The success of such an all-party government can best be ensured if the same principles of proportionality and inclusivity are also regarded as being fundamental to its decision-making as well, which takes us back to the first chapter.

# CHAPTER 3

## A COMPARATIVE CONCLUSION

Having looked at most of the more common voting procedures, the least we should do is summarise our conclusions and offer a simple comparison of them all.

Well some decision-making processes are adversarial and may cause alienation while others are far more inclusive; some voting procedures consider only the first preferences while others allow the voter a considerable degree of choice; some electoral systems are very majoritarian while others are proportional to a degree. It is all a little complex but nevertheless worth a try.

In the first decision-making table shown opposite, majoritarian methodologies are shown in tint, with the more divisive forms in the darker shade. In the second display on electoral systems overleaf, the tinted columns represent those systems which have a high threshold. Needless to say, the threshold of any system operating in a multi-member constituency depends on how many seats are in that constituency, so in the particular instances included in the diagram, each is accompanied where possible by a known example and its corresponding threshold.[1]

Two-tier systems are left untinted if as is the case here, the second tier has a low threshold, and it is this overall figure which is quoted. Approval voting gives a lower threshold to the middle-of-the-road candidate, and a higher one to the more extreme, so this one is shown hatched.

Finally, I hope the reader will accept that the concept of a threshold does not really apply to the preferendum, so this is shown in reverse. After all, an option or candidate may gain some points from everybody. Accordingly, even if the decision taken enjoys a level of consensus of only 75%, it may nevertheless enjoy 100% participation; meanwhile, in an election, although the chosen candidate may not receive the maximum possible score, she can still know that every voter has contributed to her election, and that she will be able to act as a representative for everyone in the constituency. It is, indeed, an inclusive system.

# DECISION-MAKING PROCESSES - A COMPARISON

| Voting for | 1st prefs only (EXCLUSIVE) | some prefs | all prefs (INCLUSIVE) |
|---|---|---|---|
| One of two options (RESTRICTIVE) | **simple majority** / consociational / weighted | | |
| One of some options (RESTRICTIVE) | **plurality** | | |
| One or some of all options (VOTERS' CHOICE) | | two-round majority vote / alternative vote / Finnish model[2] / approval voting | |
| One, some or all of all options (PLURALIST) | | | Condorcet / preferendum |

# ELECTORAL SYSTEMS - A COMPARISON

High threshold ●
Low threshold ○

| | 1st prefs only (EXCLUSIVE) | some preferences (INCLUSIVE) | all prefs (INCLUSIVE) |
|---|---|---|---|
| **One party only** (RESTRICTIVE) | first-past-the-post UK - 35% / Two-round France 35% / AMS | | |
| **One candidate of one party in one or two votes** (RESTRICTIVE) | PR-list Israel 1% | mixed majority & PR-list Croatia 35% & 1.4% / PR-list The Netherlands 0.7% / MMP Germany 5% / two-tier PR-list Sweden 4% | |
| **One or some candidates of one or some party/ies** (VOTERS' CHOICE) | | AV Australia 35% / approval voting / PR-STV Ireland 17% | AV + top-up / PR-list Switzerland 8.5% / PR-STV + top-up Malta 1% |
| **One, some, or all candidates of any or all parties** (PLURALIST) | | | Condorcet / preferendum / QBS / QBS + top-up |

Voting for

COUNTING PROCEDURE

In the most exclusive systems, the choice of option or candidate is restricted to two, and if neither is to the voter's liking, such 'democratic' votes are little more than a Hobson's choice.

The degree of pluralism improves when first-past-the-post is replaced by an Israeli-style PR-list system, for example. For this reason, looking at the diagram opposite, the latter is shown to the right of, and higher than, the UK's first-past-the-post.

In similar fashion, the 'some preferences' rows also vary from bottom to top. In France's two-round elections, the supporter of a minority candidate may vote for that person in the first round and, as it were, express a 2nd preference in the second round. In PR-STV, however, she may express many preferences, (although as we know, maybe only some of them will be taken into account). Accordingly, these latter systems are in the top rows of the 'some preferences' section.

Decision-making processes may also be compared in this way, and the alternative vote, for instance, allows the voter more choice of expression than does the two-round vote, so again, the former is to the right of the latter.

The clear conclusion from both comparisons is that the preferendum is more inclusive. As we know, the simple majority vote is so restrictive, it may leave up to 49% of the voters alienated from the outcome, and an even greater number alienated from, and by, the democratic process. The preferendum, on the other hand, may actually allow all the voters to have a positive influence on the outcome.

In elections, especially in lands torn by ethnic or religious division, the principle of proportionality must be paramount. Such societies should therefore use QBS, but those which can relish diversity may prefer the preferendum.

As far as decision-making is concerned, though, in deliberative poll or binding vote, the preferendum is the best. Furthermore, it may be used in all societies, and even in attempting to resolve the most bitter of disputes. It requires those concerned to view politics, not as might be inferred from Karl von Clausewitz' epithet as war by another means, not in other words as an adversarial contest, but rather as a mechanism by which at least an accommodation may be achieved, often a consensus, and at best a confluence, a collective wisdom far more comprehensive than the sum of its parts.

# Appendix I

## AN IRRELEVANT ALTERNATIVE
## AND OTHER POSSIBLE WEAKNESSES OF THE PREFERENDUM

Consider the situation when seven punters vote on four options - 'W, X, Y and Z' as follows:

| No of voters | 3 | 2 | 2 |
|---|---|---|---|
| 1st  pref | W | X | Y |
| 2nd pref | X | Y | Z |
| 3rd pref | Y | Z | W |
| 4th pref | Z | W | X |

In this instance, the preferendum scores are 'W = 18, X = 19, Y = 20 and Z = 13', so 'Y' is the most popular.

Well all seven punters think 'Y' is better than 'Z', so we could say 'Z' is actually irrelevant. Let us now, therefore, remove this irrelevance from the ballot paper, in which case, the results are like this:

| No of voters | 3 | 2 | 2 |
|---|---|---|---|
| 1st  pref | W | X | Y |
| 2nd pref | X | Y | W |
| 3rd pref | Y | W | X |

And now the preferendum scores are 'W = 15, X = 14 and Y = 13', so 'Y' is now the least popular. What's more, the order of success in the first ballot was 'Y, X, W and Z' but with 'Z' removed, the order of the remaining three is reversed into 'W, X, Y'! By any scratch of the head, that is extraordinary.

In other words, the inclusion of an irrelevant alternative may affect the outcome, which is why the preliminary stages of a preferendum, the debate and the setting of the questions, are so important. Otherwise, come the vote and substituting candidates for options, 'Y' *"has got a strong incentive to bribe 'Z' to stand, and candidate 'W' an equal incentive to bribe her to withdraw. Lucky 'Z' has found an easy way to make money, but everybody else is left to ponder on the problem of strategic manipulation."*[1]

This is often considered to be the most serious defect of a Borda count and preferendum, and the criticism is indeed fair. The preferendum, however, is not that vulnerable for, as mentioned in the text, a decision should not be enacted unless it enjoys a level of consensus of at least 75%. That's one safeguard.

Secondly, the reader may be interested to know, (if indeed you have not already guessed), that in both of the above examples, there is yet again a paradox of voting. In the first example, 'W' is more popular than 'X' by 5 votes to 2, so 'W > X', and in all, 'W > X > Y > Z > W', while in the second example, 'W > X > Y > W'. We suggested in the text that a Borda preferendum outcome is best confirmed by a Condorcet count, and that would be a second safeguard.

## MANIPULATION

In theory, *"Borda counts [and the preferendum] are very vulnerable to manipulation,"* and if you, dear reader, were intent on such devilment, you could either try to slip in a 'Z'-type irrelevant alternative, as above, or you could go for a straight tactical vote, as follows. *"If you think that most people think that your favourite candidate is about 3rd best, your most dangerous rivals are the candidates that most people think are 2nd best and 4th best. If you really want your candidate to win, your interest lies in putting these rivals at the bottom of your ranking, whatever you really think of them."*[2]

In theory, yes, that is true. But in practice, if our DUP supporter knows his candidate is 3rd, and reckons those UUP candidates are 2nd and 4th, is he really going to put them below SF and the SDLP in the hope of getting his own candidate elected?

The risk in any decision-making vote is quite large, for the final answer may well be a composite of the first two or three options; and the risk in an election is also considerable, for in a consensus democracy, every election should involve more than one representative.[3] Furthermore, if the Borda preferendum is being used in QBS in what is therefore a proportional election, such manipulations by that DUP supporter would be even more problematic!

In theory, yes, the preferendum is manipulable; but in reality, it may often encourage the more intransigent to be a little conciliatory. There will always be those who will try to manipulate any and every voting procedure; that goes without saying; but those who do so with the preferendum will find the task really quite difficult.

According to some observers (though not this author), there is one other possible disadvantage of the Borda preferendum, and that is its occasional inability to present the Condorcet winner as its final outcome. Take the example first argued by Rev. Dodgson:[4]

| No of voters | 3 | 3 | 3 | 2 |
|---|---|---|---|---|
| 1st pref | B | B | A | A |
| 2nd pref | A | A | C | D |
| 3rd pref | C | D | D | C |
| 4th pref | D | C | B | B |

in which case, the preferendum scores are:

A = 38,        B = 29,        C = 22    &    D = 21

which suggests 'A' is the winner, but the Condorcet count presents a different picture, with victory to 'B':

| | A | B | C | D | wins |
|---|---|---|---|---|---|
| A | | 5 | 11 | 11 | 2 |
| B | 6 | | 6 | 6 | 3 |
| C | 0 | 5 | | 6 | 1 |
| D | 0 | 5 | 5 | | 0 |

This anomaly is caused by the fact that 'B' wins its three Condorcet pairings by the narrowest of margins, while when 'A' beats 'C and D', it does so by the largest possible extent. On most occasions, therefore, a Condorcet count will indeed confirm the prominence of the preferendum winners, and on those occasions where there is a difference, it is well to remember that an underlying principle of an inclusive democracy is not the dominance of a majority, but the participation and satisfaction of the greatest possible number.

# Appendix II

## QBS - A Possible Weakness

In my introduction, I asked if anyone ever finds an example of QBS which does not work, to let me know. Here is one example I found myself, and you will see it is a variation of the example we used in the main text.

Consider an electorate of 100 electing 3 representatives from a choice of 6 candidates - 'A, B, C, D, E and F' - and a voting profile as shown:

| Preferences | 40 | 3 | 19 | 11 | 14 | 13 | Points | |
|---|---|---|---|---|---|---|---|---|
| 1st pref | A | F | B | E | C | D | 6 | points |
| 2nd pref | F | D | E | B | D | C | 5 | points |
| | D | A | F | F | F | F | 4 | points |
| | C | E | C | A | B | B | 3 | points |
| | E | C | A | C | E | E | 2 | points |
| | B | B | D | D | A | A | 1 | point |

The quota in this case is 100 {the valid vote} divided by 4, {the number of seats plus 1}, plus 1, which is 26, so 'A' gets elected in the 1st round.

With preferendum scores of:

'A = 350, B = 293, C = 354, D = 353, E = 304 and F = 446',

we proceed to the 2nd stage: 'B and E' reach the quota with a combined total of 30 (tinted) 1st preferences, so 'E' gets elected; and the (less tinted) 'C and D' have 27, so 'C' gets elected.

Thus 'F', with by far the largest preferendum score, remains unelected, which seems a bit rough. There again, 'F' only gets three 1st preferences and, given the fact that she is such a reasonable sort of candidate, for how else would she get the 2nd or 3rd preferences of all the other candidates, maybe she will accept this somewhat unfortunate result.

For many societies, the most important factor is proportionality, and it is because QBS gives priority to the quota over the preference that poor old 'F' loses out. A different system not yet invented could possibly redress this, but that would then leave 'C' without a seat, and to deprive one third of society of its proportional representation may not be advisable. For the moment at least, therefore, QBS will do. And I await your examples.

# Appendix III

## THE DIVISIVE REFERENDUM

To use Vernon Bogdanor's phrase, the majority vote referendum is *"a blunt instrument"*. A pretty rotten example occurred in 1991 in the old Soviet Union when Gorbachev tried to show that a majority of its inhabitants was in favour of that Union. Few asked if, in a land of umpteen minorities, such a voting procedure was 'democratic' or not - in Stalin's day, there were about 60 recognised ethnic groups, but in more recent times and with the advent of *'glasnost'*, most acknowledge about 120 nationalities. Of the 15 republics which comprised the USSR, only nine participated, and of those, only four did not change the question! Nevertheless, it was claimed that from a population of 188 million voters, 136 million voted, and 105 of them said *'Da'*. The vote meant nothing.

Another divisive issue concerned the 1986 divorce referendum in Ireland. A compromise was waiting to be found, but because the government used the uncompromising majority vote, the particular compromise it itself proposed was seen as an extreme option, at least by its more extreme opponents. The debate thus became a battle between 'divorce on demand' versus 'divorce not never no how', and a most bitter campaign ensued. If, furthermore, someone wanted to allow divorce in cases of child abuse only, he/she was in effect disenfranchised. Of those who voted, 63% said no.

Now if you don't get the answer you want, you just wait a few years and try again. In 1995, the government did exactly that, with yet another, yes-or-no vote. By an act of God perhaps - the sun was shining in Dublin but the heavens opened out west - a majority of 50.3% won the day, with only 9,100 votes between the winners and the losers. *"The people have spoken,"* said the then Taoiseach. Well, he spoke.

Quebec was far more serious, for their question concerned nationalism: in a word, do you want to be French or English? So, in another word, anyone who was not *"ethnically clean"* was disenfranchised. In their referendum 59.5% opposed the idea of separation, so that, in 1980, was that.

Then again, that was not that. In 1995, they decided to have another go. The day of the vote was first postponed as those who chose the question - my God, what power they have - decided to use a softer turn of phrase, for they were worried they might lose... which is exactly what happened, by 50.6% to 49.4% on a 93% turnout. So that is definitely that, you might think. It should be, *mais ce n'est pas vrai.*

In the wake of that vote, Quebec premier Parizeau blamed the ethnic vote, but just as the Irish referendum could not consider any 3rd opinion, so too the Quebec ballot just ignored any other aspiration, and any other people who might have held such an aspiration, like the Cree Indians. The latter therefore held their own referendum a week earlier and 96% of them voted to stay in Canada. It seems the instrument which is meant to facilitate the resolution of a question, only serves to exacerbate it.

Indeed, in some cases, the very use of the referendum has actually provoked certain persons to decry the democratic process, and others to initiate horrible acts of violence. *"The referendum as at present contemplated is an empty exercise."* With such words, the SDLP chose to boycott the 1973 border poll, and quite right too! But those words could be applied, by one side or the other, to almost any referendum, especially if used in a conflict situation. In the event, 59% voted, i.e., the Protestants, and of those, 97% said yes.

In theory, there was going to be another referendum after a further decade of misery and majoritarian mayhem, but it never happened. What eventually did happen, however, was the publication of the Framework Documents, the lesson still unlearnt. NI can stay in the United Kingdom, it says, if that is *"the present wish of a majority of its people"*, (para 18), or it can join a united Ireland *"If a majority of the people [so] wish"*, (para 17).

The documents were hailed, worldwide. Yet those very paragraphs are a source of conflict! Consider, if you would, a ridiculous scenario, for there may well come a time, after further demographic changes, when Seamus has his eighteenth birthday, and there will then be a majority of 50% + 1 in favour of a united Ireland. Unless, that is, Sammy gets his gun and kills a taig. The governments call it a peace process! God help us all.

If self-determination is to be exercised by a majority vote, any ethnic tensions in society may well be exacerbated. In Yugoslavia, for example, the use of the referendum has been nothing less than tragic:

| DATE | PLACE | ISSUE | TURNOUT | FOR OR AGAINST | RESULT |
|---|---|---|---|---|---|
| 23.12.90 | Slovenia[1] | Independence | 94% | 95% | Accepted by Slovenia, not by Serbia; war in June '91. |
| 12.05.91 Meanwhile: | Krajina[2] | Stay in FRY[3] | 95% | 90% | Ignored by Croatia; accepted by Serbia. |
| 19.05.91 | Croatia[4] | Independence | 84% | 93% | Accepted by Croatia, but neither in the Krajina nor in Serbia. Hence the war in Aug, 1991. |
| 22.10.91 | Kosova[5] | Independence | 87% | 99% | Ignored by Serbia. |
| 11.03 92 | Bosnia[6] | Independence | 63% | 99% | War. |
| 11.10.92 | Serbia | Early vote[7] | 46% | 95% | Declared invalid.[8] |
| 15.03.93 & 28.08.94 | Republika Srpska | Vance-Owen Contact Group plan | - | 96% & 90% | Karadžić used these polls in his rump enclave to thus further the war. |

# Appendix V

## THE DEBATE

To see how useless current procedures are, consider a fairly standard political debate - the sort which plague party political conferences - where there is a motion, a 1st amendment, an addendum to that 1st amendment, and a 2nd amendment. There are, then, five possibilities:

| | |
|---|---|
| A | the original motion, |
| B | the motion amended by the 1st amendment, |
| C | the motion amended by the 1st amendment and the addendum, |
| D | the motion amended by the 2nd amendment, and |
| E | nothing, *or status quo ante.* |

And just to keep the mathematics simple, let us assume only three people are in the conference centre, Ms/rs J, K and L, and that their preferences are as follows:

| | J | K | L |
|---|---|---|---|
| 1st pref | B | D | E |
| 2nd pref | C | B | C |
| 3rd pref | A | C | A |
| 4th pref | D | A | D |
| 5th pref | E | E | B |

Well according to those same old rules of debate we mentioned, the procedure is this:

i) we first debate the addendum to the 1st amendment;

ii) next we choose between the 1st amendment with or without the addendum and the 2nd amendment;

iii) having selected the preferred amendment, we then decide on whether or not we want to use it on the motion, and finally,

iv) this substantive motion, (the original motion or the motion with the preferred amendment) is put to the vote, and that's the answer.

In knock-out form, it looks like this:

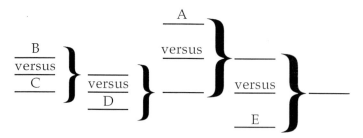

In our own example, according to the above preferences of the three voters, 'B' is more popular than 'C', 'D' is more popular than 'B', and so on; with much waving of order papers and countless work for the tellers, the debate proceeds as follows:

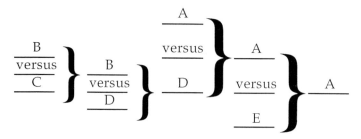

and 'A', the motion unamended, is passed.

But now let's look back at those preferences: all three voters prefer 'C' to 'A' and yet 'A' wins! Binary decision-making, majority voting, literally does not work!

And that's when people are nice; what happens in the smoke filled corridors of political power, where wheeling and dealing and high-pressure lobbying leads to vote-trading and tactical voting, can only be called chaotic... or as others pretend, democratic.

This example is adapted from p 74 of *"Liberalism Against Populism"* by Riker, 1982, by W.H Freeman and Company. Used with permission.

# Appendix V

## MONOTONICITY AND STV

Consider an electorate of 77 persons electing three representatives with, therefore, a quota of 20; and let us assume they vote like this:

| No of voters | 19 | 18 | 15 | 12 | 3 | 10 |
|---|---|---|---|---|---|---|
| 1st pref | A | B | C | D | E | E |
| 2nd pref | B | D | E | C | C | A |
| 3rd pref | D | - | - | E | - | B |
| 4th pref | - | - | - | - | - | D |

In this case, a PR-STV count will proceed as follows:

| | 1st count | 2nd count | 3rd count | |
|---|---|---|---|---|
| A | 19 | = 19 | = 19 | ✓ |
| B | 18 | = 18 | = 18 | |
| C | 15 | + 12 = 27 ✓ | - 7 = | |
| D | 12 | - 12 = - | | |
| E | 13 | 13 | + 7 = 20 ✓ | |
| | eliminate D | elect C | elect E | elect A on default. |

But imagine what happens if two of the three punters who voted 'E, C' choose to vote 'C, E' instead. The voting profile is now like this:

| No of voters | 19 | 18 | 17 | 12 | 1 | 10 |
|---|---|---|---|---|---|---|
| 1st pref | A | B | C | D | E | E |
| 2nd pref | B | D | E | C | C | A |
| 3rd pref | D | - | - | E | - | B |
| 4th pref | - | - | - | - | - | D |

and the count as shown overleaf:

|  | 1st count | 2nd count | 3rd count | 4th count |
|---|---|---|---|---|
| A | 19 | + 10 = 29 ✓ | - 9 = | |
| B | 18 | = 18 | + 9 = 27 ✓ | - 7 = |
| C | 17 | + 1 = 18 | = 18 | = 18 |
| D | 12 | = 12 | = 12 | + 7 = 19 ✓ |
| E | 11 | - 11 = - | | |
|  | eliminate E | elect A | elect B | elect D on default |

In the first example, 'C, E and A' are elected; in the second, 'A, B and D' are successful. In other words, 'C' has become more popular and yet less successful. With 15 in number 1st preferences he gets elected, but when he gets 17, he loses! Furthermore, in adjusting their preferences for 'C and E', these two punters have affected the careers of 'B and D'! It is, indeed, an extraordinary state of affairs.

In the language of the psephologist, STV is not monotonic; the preferendum, however, is. This property can be defined quite easily as follows: if an option or candidate becomes more popular with the electorate, it/he/she should then have a greater chance of success. Neither STV nor the two-round majority vote can always guarantee this property.

For a much fuller treatment of this subject, please see Dummett, 1997, pp 99-103.

# APPENDIX VI - THE PREFERENDUM FLOW CHART

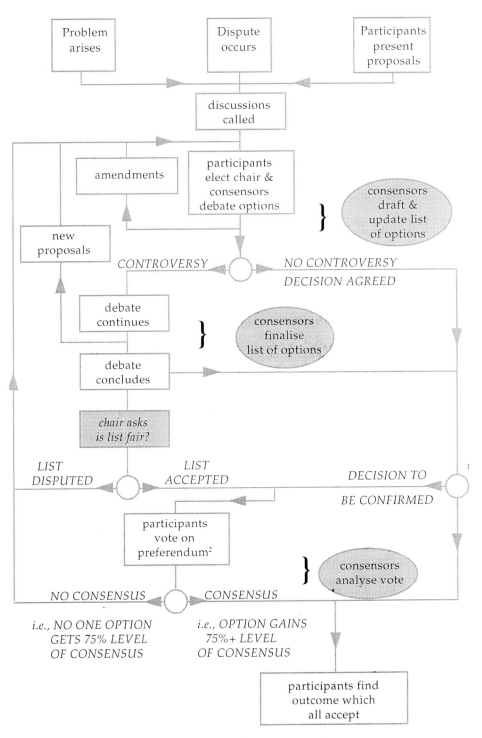

# NOTES

1 According to Art. 21 of the 1948 United Nations Declaration of Human Rights:

   I    *Everyone has the right to take part in the government of his country, directly or through freely elected representatives.*

 III   *The will of the people shall be the basis of the authority of the government; this shall be expressed in periodic and genuine elections which shall be held by secret vote or by equivalent free voting procedures.*

2 *"Report of the Constitution Review Group"*, p 398. This mighty volume was published by the Government of Ireland in 1996 and submitted to the Oireachtas (the two Houses of the Irish Parliament) in May of that year.

3 McLean, 1989, p 34.

4 Rule 19 of its 1961 version, para c), quoted in McLean, *ibid*, p 28, and how strange it is that one who is so critical of Soviet majoritarianism can be so supportive of its western equivalent.

5 The Guardian, 30.4.94.

6 Dummett, 1997, p 32. It is interesting to note in this regard that many Africans were utterly confused when their colonial masters suggested they should employ *"a loyal opposition"*. To impose such a binary system in lands split on a tribal basis was at least unwise, and no wonder Julius Nyerere and others quickly replaced the two-party system by a more cohesive, one-party arrangement... which is what the British also did during the Great Depression and WWII.

7 This statement was propounded by the National Republican Movement for Development and Democracy (sic) and its more extreme offshoot, the Coalition for Defence of the Republic. Quoted in The Guardian, 11.9.94.

8 In 1958, he published that which has come to be seen as a classic, *"The Theory of Committees and Elections"*. Other economists have since joined the field, most notably Kenneth Arrow, and only more recently have political scientists like Iain McLean entered the debate.

9 The term *'preferendum'* was first coined at a 1984 meeting of the European Greens in Dover, though I first advocated this decision-making process in a letter to the *Irish News* on 3rd May, 1977. I must confess that at the time, I did not realise that the basis of the preferendum count had been invented over a hundred years previously by a certain Rev. Dodgson. He, unfortunately, forgot to write a book about it and wrote *"Alice in Wonderland"* instead. He was, indeed, Lewis Carroll. But he too had not known that in 1784, the same methodology had actually been proposed to and adopted by the French Academy of Sciences on the recommendations of a M. Jean-Charles de Borda. Hence the Borda count.

    And even he, it seems, had not been aware of its earlier discovery by Nicholas Cusanus or Nicholas of Cusa, a canon lawyer of the fifteenth century. In his system, especially proposed for the election of the pope, *"each of the electors [is to] get a ballot with the name of each candidate on it. [The elector] puts after each name on the paper a number ranging between 1 and the total number of candidates, in the order of ascending merit. Thus if there are 10 candidates, the best would have the number 10 after his name, and the worst would be number 1. Then all the ballots are put into a sack, and a priest, having said Mass, takes them out one by one, recording the number next to each name. The candidate who gets the highest number of votes, when all are totalled, is elected."*

Well that sounds pretty good to me, for with the exception of the rule about Holy Mass, it is in fact an exact definition of the preferendum count, whereas in this instance, a Borda count would use a points scale of 9 to 0. Like the current author, Nicholas was loud in his own praise of his own invention. *"With much study, I have not been able to find a safer system and believe me, no more perfect system can be found."* Sigmund, 1963, p 212. Copyright © 1963 by the President and Fellows of Harvard College, reprinted by permission of Harvard University Press.

10 See *"An Analysis of the Results of the NI Forum Elections"*, Emerson, 1996.

11 See Emerson, 1994, pp 89 *et seq.*.

12 At first sight, this may appear to be a rather arbitrary figure, roughly midway between the 100% of total unanimity and the 50% + 1 unanimity of a minimum majority. In fact, of course, it is a percentage which refers not to a number of people, but to the level of enthusiasm with which *everyone* regards the option concerned. What's more, experience suggests a level of consensus of 75% is both desirable and attainable, but please see *ibid.*, p 31 *et seq.*.

## NOTES ON CHAPTER 1

**1** Options are often seen as mutually exclusive, as in the very simple example of a swimming pool: either it opens on Sundays, or it does not open. It is, as they say, a clear choice, yes-or-no! If, however, the question is asked differently - what, if any, will be the pool's working routine on Sundays? - if in other words, the debate is more sophisticated, compromise options will actually be forthcoming.

Similarly, on the constitution, we could ask if Northern Ireland is British or Irish? But that, may I suggest, is unfair. It would be much wiser to discuss the question of whether Northern Ireland could be administered by, devolved within, federated with, independent of, or integrated into, the regions and/or nations of either Britain and/or the Republic of Ireland. That is at least seven options already, and we have not yet even mentioned the EU.

**2** See, for instance, Lord Citrine's *"ABC of chairmanship"* where he writes, *"If an amendment be carried, it displaces the Original Motion and becomes the substantive motion ... [and this] shall [then] be put to the vote."* Quoted in McLean, 1989, p 46.

**3** For a fuller treatment of this subject, see Farquharson's fascinating work, 1969.

**4** See Emerson, 1994, p 113.

**5** *"The speaker's rules in the Finnish parliament require that when a vote is taken over a set of alternatives, the first ballot is taken between the two alternatives furthest apart."* Nurmi, 1987, p 163. A similar methodology is used in Norway; McLean, 1989, p 8.

6   A case history taken from McLean, 1989, p 47, but it is also featured in Farquharson, 1969, and Riker, 1982.

   Minority endorsement sounds like a nice idea. If, however, it too is to be effected by a majority vote, then maybe only a majority of the minority will endorse the majority view, so the minority of the minority would then have to endorse the endorsement... by another majority vote. And so on. When taken to its logical conclusion, a majority of a minority of a minority... of a minority of the minority, i.e., two people, could veto the lot!

7   For a more detailed appraisal of these arguments, see Riker, 1982, p 192.

8   As far as I know, weighted majority voting was first used in 1179, when the two-thirds rule was introduced for the election of the pope... but whether that rule was itself introduced by a simple or weighted majority vote, I know not! Sigmund, 1963, p 74.

9   The main difference between a Borda and a preferendum count is that, in an $n$-option ballot, the Borda count is based on a points scale of $\{(n-1)\ to\ 0\}$, whereas in the preferendum, the scale is $\{n\ to\ 1\}$. The outcome, of course, is unaffected by this change, but the implications for the rules of partial voting are considerable.

10  The Opsahl report, a citizens' inquiry into the political situation of Northern Ireland, failed to consider the preferendum as a decision-making process. Instead it opted for a consociational voting system in a concept which is now a well-worn cliché, parity of esteem.

   Many an observer would agree with fair employment agencies, with parity of languages, with both flags flying from the City Hall, and so forth, but to suggest society should be divided into two (electoral registers) and that both 'halves' should have, in effect, parity of veto, is almost bound to lead to a stalemate. As one wit observed in the Dublin Forum for Peace and Reconciliation, this would compound the indecisiveness of Belfast City Hall and produce only parity of steam!

11  Fortnight Educational Trust's *"Separation or Sharing"*, (Dec. 1996).

12  If $L_C$ is the level of consensus enjoyed by option 'C', if $L_D$ is the level of option 'D', and $L_{CD}$ the level of the composite, then $L_{CD}$ is defined by the following equation:

$$L_{CD} = L_C + (100 - L_C) \times L_D \text{ (see Emerson, 1994, p 86).}$$

13  *"World Orders, Old and New"* by Noam Chomsky, p 36.

14  Democratic decision-making is a question of choice. To take a very simple example, we as a society have to make up our minds as to whether we drive on the left hand side or the right, to quote one of the very few truly two-option questions we have to face. On more complex matters, we must also decide which economic policies should prevail, and so on. Whether the range of options is limited to two or whether there are more *"on the table"*, it is still a question of choice. If our 1st preference is not obtainable, perhaps we must settle for a 2nd or 3rd choice. If chips are off, love, you had better have mashed; it's that or go hungry.

   In other words, it matters not a lot whether a voter thinks his/her 1st choice is far superior to his 2nd, or only marginally so, it is all, still, a question of choice, and voters should be asked to state their preferences on the basis that, if it cannot be the 1st, then let it be the 2nd, and so on. In the jargon of the psephologist, preferences should be ordinal, or the utility function of any preference voting system should be 1, and arguments as to whether or not the punter feels his 1st preference is 7 or 7 times 77 times better than his 2nd choice are irrelevant.

Because in all fields of social choice, we must make a decision one way or the other, this book considers only ordinal preference profiles and apart from approval voting, does not consider those procedural variations of other decision-making processes or electoral systems which allow the punter to bracket two or more options/candidates as equal preferences. And thank heavens for that, for otherwise this book would be twice as long and three times as full of sums!

15  In the first round, Yeltsin, Zyuganov and Lebed got 35%, 32% and 14% respectively, and the seven other candidates shared 15%. In the second round, Yeltsin won 54% to Zyuganov's 40%.

16  See, for example, Dr. Asbjorn Eide's submission to the Dublin Forum for Peace and Reconciliation where he states (p 10), *"weighted voting... could block decision-making altogether."*

17  *"Long Walk to Freedom"* by Nelson Mandela, p 714.

18  *"Facts on File"*, 1991, p 225; indeed, according to the opinion polls, a majority of Slovaks wanted to retain the Czechoslovak nation, and only the politicians were at odds. It was definitely another clear-cut case for a multi-option poll.

19  *"The Fall of Yugoslavia"* by Misha Glenny, Penguin, 1982, p 18.

20  Nurmi, 1987, p 57. Or take another quotation: *"approval voting is somewhere between plurality voting and the Borda count"*. Riker, 1982, p 89.

21  This was a conclusion of the *"Where Lies the Compromise?"* conference of May, 1995 - see bibliography - and similar conclusions have also come about as a result of empirical research elsewhere, cf. Van Neenhizen, 1992. Interestingly enough, there are those who, knowing Condorcet to be frail at times, recommend the additional use of a Borda count. QED. (And see note 6 on p 95.)

22  See, for example, p 10 of Dr. Asbjorn Eide's submission to the Dublin Forum for Peace and Reconciliation: *"Pure majoritarian governance in divided societies constitutes a serious threat to group accommodation. This is now widely recognised."*

23  The first of three *"People's Conventions"* in 1986 was attended by over 200 people, and they included members of the UUP and others of SF, and even some of Ulster Clubs!

*"The Other Talks"*, 1991, a 1993 conference on power-sharing, and the 1995 *"Where Lies the Compromise?"* conference are described in the bibliography.

A 1996 *"Citizens' Assembly"* brought together members of SF and the DUP, etc..

The author has conducted other practical demonstrations in Cork, Dublin, Edinburgh, Moscow and Sofia.

24  Dummett, 1997, p 71.

25  See, for example, Prof. Donald Saari who writes: *"Among other positive features of the Borda count... it is the unique method... to minimise the likelihood that a small group can successfully manipulate the outcome."* Saari, 1995, p 14.

26  The parallel between the SDLP and Radovan Karadžić's rebel Bosnian Serbs cannot of course be taken any further; the former has always eschewed violence, the latter have committed the very worst forms of atrocities. See also Appendix III.

27  Black, 1958, p 182.

28  For a fuller description of levels of consensus, see Emerson, 1994, (and cf. note 12 on p 92).

29  In theory, (first formulated by Kenneth Arrow in his *"Social Choice and Individual Values"*, 1963) and known as his *"General Possibility Theorem"*, no voting procedure is perfect, neither in decision-making nor in elections. He first laid down a number of conditions of fairness, and these include the following:

UNIVERSAL CONDITION
there should be no restriction on the voters' choice, so (according to this author), that's majority voting out the window;

MONOTONICITY
more popular options/candidates should be more likely to win, which is a blow to STV;

INDEPENDENCE FROM IRRELEVANT ALTERNATIVES
the inclusion on the ballot paper of spurious options/candidates should not affect the overall popularity of the others, and that knocks the Borda preferendum for five;

CITIZENS' SOVEREIGNTY, ANONYMITY, THE PARETO CONDITION AND NON-DICTATORSHIP
suggest that every vote should be treated equally and that what the voters want they should actually get.

In all, he suggested four conditions necessary for a perfect procedure, and then went on to prove that no one voting mechanism will satisfy them all. The mathematical proofs by Arrow, 1963, Pattanaik, 1971, and others are all a little complicated, so may I recommend either Sen, 1970, who can still be fairly difficult, or the easier discussions in Riker, 1982, and McLean, 1989.

## NOTES ON CHAPTER 2

1  In French parliamentary elections, the second round vote will be a *'triangulaire'* if in the 1st round each of three candidates manages to get more than 12.5%.

2  The German MMP system is actually a two-tier system in which the voter has two votes; the first is a plurality vote for a constituency representative, and the second is a PR-list vote. AMS, on the other hand, is not so good, for it gives the voter just the one vote, and bases the second part top-up on that first round vote.

The British government has recently announced a form of the German system for the new devolved assemblies in Scotland and Wales - see *"Scotland's Parliament"*, Annex C, HMSO, July 1997, for example.

Furthermore, it is intending to reform its first-past-the-post general election system. In theory, an 'Independent Commission on the Voting System' under Lord

Jenkins will initiate a period of public consultation. In practice, however, the decision to adopt a two-tier MMP system has probably already been taken. There will be a referendum, of course, but as we know from Chapter 1, any use of a two-option poll in what is so obviously a multi-option debate is usually just a form of manipulation.

3   A Fianna Fail deputy, Mr. Noel Dempsey TD, has recently put forward such a proposal; see *The Irish Times*, 13.1.97, 22.2.97 and 21.6.97.

4   Brams and Fishburn, 1983, p 14.

5   The name given to the Moscow headquarters of the old KGB, the 'committee of state security' or *'komitet gosudarstvennoj byezopastnosti'*.

6   Many have recognised that there is a strong possibility of a cycle whenever the Condorcet method is used, and some observers - Dodgson (who suggested resort to a Borda count), Black and Copeland, amongst others - have proposed certain rules to be used on such occasions, in order to get the fairest possible outcome; on balance, though, *"There is no good reason... for preferring one set of rules to another, yet they can lead to different outcomes."* Riker, 1982, p 76.

7   In the first count, 'A' with 40 1st preferences gains the quota with a surplus of 19 votes, and these are transferred to '$A_1$'.

     In the second count with no-one reaching the quota, we eliminate 'F's vote of 5, and these are transferred to their 2nd preference, 'D'.

     In the third count, we eliminate the next smallest score, namely 'E's 11, and the latter all gave 'B' their 2nd preference.

     'B' thus gets a fourth count score of 30 so she is elected. Her surplus of 9 votes (30 minus the quota, 21) is now transferred in accordance with the wishes of all 30 voters. The 19 voters who gave 'B' their 1st preference gave their 2nd to 'E' (but 'E' has already been eliminated), their 3rd preference to 'F' (and 'F' has also been eliminated) and their 4th to 'C', so 'C' gets:

$$\frac{19}{30} \text{ of the surplus, and } \frac{19}{30} \times 9 = 5.7$$

     The other 11 voters who gave 'B' a fourth count score of 30 were the 11 who gave their 1st preferences to 'E', and while their 3rd preference goes to 'F' (eliminated) and their 4th to 'A' (elected), their 5th preference goes to '$A_1$', so '$A_1$' gets:

$$\frac{11}{30} \times 9 = 3.3$$

     '$A_1$' now gets the quota with a surplus of 1.3, but even if all 1.3 votes were transferred to 'D', he would still not catch up with 'C', so she gets the final seat with a score less than the quota and therefore 'by default'.

     This count is another clear example of the complicated quirks of STV. 'F' gets 95 3rd preferences and none of them was counted. '$A_1$' gets 11 5th preferences, and these secure her election. Very odd!

8   Silber and Little, 1995, p 96. The system used was actually based on the French rather than the British form of majoritarianism: the two round variety. Tudjman got 42% of the vote in both the 1st and 2nd rounds, yet 68% of the seats. Cohen, 1995, p 100.

Croatia has now (1997) got a mixed system, part majoritarian - based on the UK's first-past-the-post system - for 24% of the seats, and part PR-list, for 70%. Unlike Germany's MMP system, however, the PR part is not designed to compensate for any disproportionality produced by the first majoritarian part. In addition, 6% of the seats are reserved for eight different ethnic groups - Hungarians, Italians, Czechs, Slovaks, Ruthenians, Ukrainians, Germans and Austrians - which does not help the Serbs very much! IDEA, 1997, p 98 and Information Service, Croatian Embassy.

9   *"The Fall of Yugoslavia"* by Misha Glenny, p 41. Serbia did actually use a system of PR, but only for the election of 'unimportant' people, like local councillors. As far as his direct power base was concerned, Milošević acted, like nearly every other politician does, in his own vested interest. (See note 15 below.)

10  Silber and Little, 1995, p 232. The Bosnian elections were part two-round and part PR, and the landslide victory for the nationalists was definitely a consequence, albeit in part, of this electoral system. The results confounded *"trends identified by many observers and public opinion polls which indicated that voters would support parties espousing non-ethnic or cross-ethnic programmes"*. Cohen, 1995, p 146.

In 1996, as part of the Dayton agreement, a PR-list system was introduced, and how sad it was to see the international community advocating a system which, because of the use of separate electoral registers and separate lists of candidates, actually promoted 'ethnic cleansing by democratic means'. (The author was an OSCE accredited observer for those elections.)

11  Ante Boban, Radovan Karadžić and Alija Izetbegović were the three leaders of the almost exclusively Bosnian Catholic, the almost exclusively Bosnian Orthodox and the mainly Bosnian Moslem parties respectively.

12  Israel also uses just the one constituency.

13  A better electoral system, PR-STV + a top-up, was proposed by the GP in its discussion document, while an analysis of the vote proved that the government had indeed devised a system which favoured the bigger parties. They always do. Is that because single-party governments find pluralism difficult to handle, I wonder? A further criticism is to be found in the Summer 1996 edition of the NI Community Relations Council's *"Journal"*.

14  A regional or national top-up based on preferendum scores would be a little complicated, because any 1st preferences would have to be given a number of points equal to the number of candidates in the most hotly contested constituency. There again, if the voters' first three party preferences only were taken into account, and if the preferendum rules for partial voting were applied, such a PR top-up could be quite easily calculated.

When therefore an 'A' party supporter votes 'A F D C E B', the 'top-up' scores will be 'A = 3, F = 2 and D = 1'. If another votes 'A F $F_1$ D C E B', the scores will again be 'A = 3, F = 2 and D = 1'. While if a third votes partially and only votes 'A F $F_1$' (in other words, voting for only two parties), the scores will be 'A = 2 and F = 1'.

If the top-up is to be applied to majority voting (as in AMS) or small constituency PR-list voting, a preferendum base is advisable; if applied to QBS, the preferendum element of QBS may make such a requirement unnecessary, and as long as the PR-list top-up constituency is sufficiently large and the threshold correspondingly small, such could well suffice.

15  In 1992, Bill Clinton received the support of *"only 24.5% of the eligible electorate, narrowly beating Woodrow Wilson in 1912 for the lowest percentage in American history"*, Fishkin, 1995, p 47.

In 1979, Margaret Thatcher won the British general election with the support of only 33% of the electorate, a lot more than that unelected dictator, the bolshevik Lenin. He won only 175 seats in the November 1917 elections as compared to the Socialist Revolutionaries who gained 410. He therefore stormed the parliament in January 1918 and took power by force of arms.

Meanwhile, talking of other, more democratic dictatorships, in Serbia in 1990, as in the USA, *"less than half the electorate voted"* and yet *"Milošević got 52% of the votes,"* 78% of the seats and 100% of the power! *"A Paper House"* by Mark Thompson, p 212.

It is sobering to recall in this regard that in July 1932, Adolf Hitler won 37% of the popular vote; *"The European Dictatorships 1918-1945"* by Stephen Lee, p 144.

16  The partial value given to the preferendum points must be balanced by a similar partial value given to the preference used for the calculation of the quota; see Emerson 1994, pp 124-6.

17  There must be lots of lovely stories to demonstrate this point; suffice here to mention just one. It happened at the time of Ireland's first referendum attempt by the major party in power to ditch PR-STV, which was of course a British invention, in favour of majority rule, another British imposition. *"The people were exhorted to vote 'Yes and de Valera', [but] a large number voted 'No and de Valera'"*. Fair play to them. Lakeman, 1970, p 248.

18  Please see Emerson, 1994, p 94 et seq..

## NOTES ON CHAPTER 3

1  Except for the Croatian example, (for which see note 8 on pp 95-6), all thresholds are taken from Lijphart, 1994.

2  See note 5 on p 91.

## NOTES ON APPENDIX I

1  This example is taken from McLean, 1987 and 1989, p 163 and p 128 respectively. See also Riker, 1982, p 92.

2  See McLean, 1989, p 58.

3  See Emerson, 1994, p 41.

4  See McLean, 1987, p 163.

## NOTES ON APPENDIX III

1   Slovenia is 87% Slovenian, the remainder being made up of over half a dozen different 'nationalities'.

2   The *'Krajina'* were three somewhat undefined bits of Croatia, about 25% of the total land area, first settled by the Serbs in 1552 and ruled then not by Croatia but directly from Vienna. The first two were overrun by Tudjman in 1995.

3   Federal Republic of Yugoslavia which now means Serbia and Montenegro.

4   Croatia's largest minority were the Serbs, some of whom - about 5% of the entire population - lived in the *krajina* where they happened to be in a majority, but more than 5% used to live in Zagreb, where of course they were in a minority.

5   Kosova is 92% Albanian. It used to be an autonomous part of Serbia, and actually has rather better claim to independence than had any *krajina*.

6   Bosnia was nominally about 40% Muslim, 30% Orthodox (Serb) and 20% Catholic (Croat); (in fact, of course, there were 27% mixed marriages, and such so-called religious-cum-ethnic divisions are, or should be and unfortunately are not, meaningless). Given that the advent of 'democracy' had facilitated the consolidation of these religious differences into three sectarian blocs or political parties, any two groups could now gang up against the other to form 'the majority'. The Muslims and Catholics voted 'for', and the Orthodox boycotted. On the day of the vote, the barricades went up in Sarajevo. Days later, the Serbs were fighting the Muslims and Croats. And one year later, the Muslims and Croats were also fighting each other.

7   This was all part of a move by the then prime minister, Panić, to get rid of Milošević...

8   ...but the shrewd Milošević was saved by a special little rule which insisted on a 50% turnout.

NB   At the same time, it must be said that the majoritarian referendum is not always so divisive, and this is especially true when conducted on a multi-optional basis. The first known example was in 1921 when Western Australia held a four-option poll on liquor licensing - see *"Asking the People"* by Allen Macartney, Edinburgh University, 1992. The most sophisticated took place in Guam in 1982, when voters had a choice of seven constitutional options - see *"Plebiscite Election"* by the Guam Election Commission. And New Zealand used an interesting innovation in 1992. They first held a non-binding 'indicative referendum' to see which of four possible electoral systems, if any, was likely to be the most popular, and then used a binding two-option ballot one year later - see *"Representation"*, Summer 1994.

## NOTES ON APPENDIX VI

1   When differences of opinion do not cause animosity between the participants, the latter may nevertheless decide to use a preferendum vote, if only to see just what is the true level of support for what may already have been agreed. See also p 4.

2   In some circumstances, participants may also want to use a preferendum straw poll to see which options deserve further study and debate.

# BIBLIOGRAPHY

ARROW, KENNETH, *"Social Choice and Individual Values"*, Yale, 1963, is the second bible of social choice theory, a small but fairly heavy work in which he describes his General Possibility Theorem.

BLACK, DUNCAN, *"The theory of Committees and Elections"*, Cambridge, 1958, is the foundation stone of modern social choice theory, and he it was who first reminded the world of the voting procedures devised by Dodgson, de Borda and Condorcet... though as he himself admits *"I was [initially] unacquainted with the earlier history of the theory and, indeed, did not know that it had a history,"* (p xi).

BOGDANOR, VERNON, *"The People and the Party System"*, Cambridge, 1981, is very good as far as it goes, but it does not reach decision-making.

BRAMS, STEVEN and FISHBURN, PETER, *"Approval Voting"*, Birkhauser,1983, compares their own chosen form of approval voting with what they know to be much worse, majority voting, but not with other forms which may be much better! They dismiss STV because of its non-monotonicity, and they ignore the Borda count because on the very rare occasion, it may not give a Condorcet winner, yet frequently nor does theirs! Altogether a most frustrating read.

COHEN, LEONARD J., *"Broken Bonds - Yugoslavia's Disintegration and Balkan Politics in Transition"*, Westview Press, 1995, is one of the few accounts of their recent wars to cover the details of any relevant elections.

§   DUMMETT, MICHAEL, *"Voting Procedures"*, OUP, 1984, explains why so many voting systems are inaccurate, and asks why so many politicians and journalists do not understand this.

§   •   *"Principles of Electoral Reform"*, OUP, 1997, is another good nail in the coffin of majoritarianism.

EMERSON, P.J., *"Northern Ireland - That Sons May Bury Their Fathers"*, LPD, 1979, in which I first proposed the preferendum and matrix vote.

•   *"Consensus Voting Systems"*, *'samizdat'* (privately published), 1991, was my first substantial work on the preferendum.

•   *"A Bosnian Perspective"*, December Publications, 1993, describes my own wartime sojourn in Bosnia.

§   •   *"The Politics of Consensus"*, *'samizdat'*, 1994, is my definitive work on both the preferendum and the matrix vote.

•   *"A Green Party/Comhaontas Glas Discussion Document"*, 1996, was a contribution to the debate on electoral systems, held as part of the multi-party talks in Stormont in January and February of that year.

- *"An Analysis of the Results of the Northern Ireland Forum Elections of May 1996"*, GP, 1996.

§ FARQUHARSON, ROBIN, *"Theory of Voting"*, New Haven, 1969, is a lovely little work on the nonsense of majority voting.

FISHKIN, JAMES S., *"The Voice of the People"*, Yale University Press, 1995. This talks of extending the democratic process via citizens' juries, focus groups and deliberative polls, but for reasons unclear, he does not mention voting procedures at all.

IDEA, THE INSTITUTE FOR DEMOCRACY AND ELECTORAL ASSISTANCE, *"The International IDEA Handbook of Electoral System Design"*, 1997, is a superb summary of all existing systems, worldwide.

LAKEMAN, ENID, *"How Democracies Vote"*, Faber and Faber, 1970, is yet another of her impassioned pleas for STV.

§ LIJPHART, AREND, *"Electoral Systems and Party Systems"*, OUP, 1994, discusses the umpteen variations on various themes of different electoral systems currently in use.

§ MCLEAN, IAIN, *"Public Choice, an Introduction"*, Blackwell, 1987, and…

§ • *"Democracy and New Technology"*, Polity Press, 1989, are two very readable discussions with but the one disadvantage: the author still believes in majority rule.

NEWENHIZEN, JILL VAN, *"The Borda method is most likely to respect the Condorcet principle"*, Economic Theory, Vol 2, 1992, pp 69-83.

§ NURMI, HANNU, *"Comparing Voting Systems"*, Dordrecht, Reidel, 1987, is a useful guide to both decision-making processes and electoral systems.

PATTANAIK, PRASANTA K., *"Voting and Collective Choice"*, Cambridge, 1971, is a complicated volume for those interested in the mathematics of social choice and welfare economics.

§ RIKER, W. H., *"Liberalism and Populism"*, W H Freeman and Co., 1982, is another excellent work which many will be pleased to note puts the more complicated mathematics into the appendices.

However, I have one disagreement: he supports the two-party system, (p 113), even though he also shows that in many such systems, both parties tend to merge as they chase the median voter, and the two-party system is, in effect, a form of one-party state.

Tony Blair, some would say, is proof positive of that! Meanwhile, in lands divided by religious or ethnic disputes, each side also tends to split into two, which is why we have the DUP and the UUP on the 'red hand', with SF and the SDLP the two shades of green. With the rise of the PUP/UDP loyalists, either the DUP or the UUP should be worried, while any other player like the UKUP will probably finish up as a poodle.

SAARI, DONALD G., *"Basic Geometry of Voting"*, Springer, 1995, is a very complicated way of praising the Borda methodology.

SEN, AMARTYA K., *"Collective Choice and Social Welfare"*, San Francisco and Edinburgh, 1970, is designed for both the literate and the numerate.

SIGMUND, PAUL E., *"Nicholas of Cusa and Mediaeval Political Thought"*, Harvard, 1963.

§   SILBER, LAURA and LITTLE, ALLAN, *"The Death of Yugoslavia"*, BBC Penguin, 1995, is a truly scholarly work of that sad tragedy.

§   Recommended reading for those not too concerned with convoluted mathematics.

---

In addition, the current author has edited the following:

*"People's Conventions"* conference reports, 1986, covers NI's first ever experiment in the preferendum, and the world's first on the matrix vote. Those attending included people from SF, the UUP, the NIO, and even Ulster Clubs!

*"The Other Talks"* conference report, 1991, refers to a meeting of SF and UUP etc., ten parties in all, with the preferendum now computerised.
   The event was witnessed by two visitors from Yugoslavia, and warnings were made about the dangers of using a two-option referendum in Bosnia.
   That vote nevertheless went ahead, in March 1992... with horrible consequences.

*"Power-sharing conference"* report, 1993, describes how councillors from SF, UUP etc., discussed and then voted on such aspects of the democratic process as gender quotas and non-majoritarian decision-making.

§   *"Where Lies the Compromise?"* conference report, 1995. This computerised experiment in decision-making involved members of SF, UUP, PUP etc., debating and then voting on the constitution; the count was conducted according to five different methodologies.

# INDEX

Asterisked items are also in the glossary.

---

Further copies of:

"Consensus Voting Systems" £ 2.50

"The Politics of Consensus" £ 12.50

"Beyond the Tyranny of the Majority" £ 7.50

and conference reports:

"The Other Talks" £ 2.00

"Power-sharing Conference" £ 1.00

"Where Lies the Compromise?" £ 2.00

are available from:

THE DE BORDA INSTITUTE
36 Ballysillan Road
Belfast BT14 7QQ
N Ireland

# THE DE BORDA INSTITUTE

For the promotion of inclusive voting procedures.

## AIMS

The de Borda Institute seeks to promote inclusive democratic procedures on all occasions of social choice, whether political or not, whether in relation to the election of representatives or concerned with the resolution of a dispute. Such voting procedures ensure that everybody contributes to the outcome in such a way that no one faction wins a victory but everyone gains the best possible compromise.

## PURPOSES

The purpose of the Institute are sevenfold:

i   to promote the development and use of inclusive decision-making processes such as the Borda preferendum (subject if need be to a Condorcet count) whenever there are matters of controversy to be resolved by groups consisting of three or more members;

ii   to offer advice as to the advantages of the Borda preferendum over other decision-making voting methodologies;

and not withstanding the Institute's declared bias in favour of the preferendum,

iii   to facilitate any group wishing to use any decision-making voting procedure in common usage.

Given that the election of representatives is often crucial to any decision-making process, the Institute shall also seek:

iv   to promote the Borda preferendum and matrix vote (combined with a PR quota in the quota Borda system) as fair electoral systems;

v   to offer advice as to which inclusive electoral system should be used on which occasion;

vi   to demonstrate how these electoral systems are superior to most other known systems;

and again not withstanding the Institute's declared bias in favour of these fairer systems,

vii   to facilitate any group wishing to use any known electoral system.

Jean Charles de Borda was born on 4th May, 1733. At the age of 23, he was elected to the Paris *Académie des Sciences,* though mainly for his work in fluid dynamics. In the years which followed, he proved himself to be not only a brilliant scientist, but also an accomplished naval officer. (On a rather more modest scale, the present author rose to the rank of first lieutenant as a submariner before teaching maths and physics in a school for the poor in Nairobi.)

The latter half of the eighteenth century was a period of great social change in Europe and the Americas, and there were many on both sides of the Atlantic who longed, not only to reject the *ancien régimes* of the monarchies, but also to adopt something better than the *"frightful abomination"* (to use George Washington's description) of the English two-party system.

Only in France, however, did *les philosophes* try to devise a more accurate decision-making methodology and two were proposed: the Borda and Condorcet systems. In 1784, the *Académie* adopted the former and it worked well.

It was abolished in 1800 by one not best known for his democratic idealism, a certain Napoleon Bonaparte.

# OTHER PUBLICATIONS ON CONSENSUS
## WRITTEN OR CONTRIBUTED TO BY THE AUTHOR

1989  *"Consensus - Democracy without Opposition"*, Moscow News No 6/89, where with Irina Bazileva, his co-author, he advocated a non-two-party, pluralist, political system for the emerging *'perestroika'* government of Russia.

1990  *"Pravo i Vlast" {"Power and the Law"}*, an anthology of contemporary Russian thought which included their article entitled *"Power, psychology and the politics of consensus"*.

1990  *"Consensus"*, where they were published alongside Alexandr Solzhenitsyn in Russia's leading literary journal, *'Novy Mir'*, No. 3/90.

1990  *"Not by the majority alone"*, *'Debaty'*, [Bulgaria's leading political weekly] No . 17/90.

\*  In addition to many articles and interviews written and/or undertaken in Northern Ireland, he has published and/or broadcast in Russia, Azerbaijan, Georgia, The Ukraine, Romania, and the former (and future) Yugoslavia, namely, in Bosnia, Croatia, Macedonia and Serbia. He has also conducted a number of experiments in the use of the preferendum and/ or matrix vote in Ireland North and South, Scotland, Russia and Bulgaria.

On a rather different theme, he has also published:

*"What an Extraordinary Title for a Travel Book"*
and
*"The Dove of Peace a'Learning How to Fly"*.